D1613729

BATTLE OF STONY CREEK.

Battle Maps

AND

Charts

OF THE

American Revolution

BATTLE OF EUTAW SPRINGS.

WASHINGTON

Battle Maps

AND

Charts

OF THE

American Revolution

WITH

EXPLANATORY NOTES

AND

SCHOOL HISTORY REFERENCES

BY

HENRY B. CARRINGTON, M. A., LL. D.

COLONEL UNITED STATES ARMY

Author of "Battles of the American Revolution"

WITH A NEW INTRODUCTION BY
GEORGE ATHAN BILLIAS

ARNO PRESS
A New York Times Company
NEW YORK   1974

1.   United States—History—Revolution, 1775-1783—
Campaigns and battles.   2.   United States—History—
Revolution, 1775-1783—Maps.   I.   Title.
E230.C322   1974   912'.1'97333   74-8018
ISBN 0-405-05540-4

Library of Congress Cataloging in Publication Data

Carrington, Henry Beebee, 1824-1912.
    Battle maps and charts of the American Revolution.
    Reprint of the ed. published by A. S. Barnes, New York.
    1.   United States—History—Revolution, 1775-1783—
Campaigns and battles.   2.   United States—History—
Revolution, 1775-1783—Maps.   I.   Title.
E230.C322   1974   912'.1'97333   74-8018
ISBN 0-405-05540-4

Introduction

by
GEORGE ATHAN BILLIAS
Clark University

"Terrain is a tyrant," a famous general once observed. What he meant was that all military operations in the final analysis are dictated by geographical considerations. The highest-ranking general is humbled by the lay of the land to which he must conform in planning his strategy and maneuvers. Henry Carrington's maps of the Revolutionary War are of significance because they reveal to us the alternatives open to the American and British generals.

The maps show America in 1775 to be a long, thin line of small communities spread mainly along the coast. There were only five cities of any size in the American wilderness — Philadelphia, Boston, New York, Charleston, and Newport — all of them ports of entry. Behind them lay few roads, and once the British Navy shut off coastal navigation no section of the country could be reached easily when marching overland. Settlements in the South were more widely dispersed than those in the North — a lesson in American geography the British general, Cornwallis, learned to his regret.

Given the scarcity of a road network, the country was divided into three natural theaters of operation — the New England, Middle, and Southern Colonies. Each could exist independently because of the decentralized nature of political authority and economic self-sufficiency of each region. British domination over one region had little or no effect on the others. The same was true of the five major cities: all were captured and occupied sometime during the war, but none proved crucial to the Patriot cause. The absence of any strategic centers in America posed a problem for the British generals charged with the responsibility of subduing the rebellious colonists — there was no vital heart whose capture would bring victory.

The vastness of the American continent and its varied nature raised other problems. Stretching more than one thousands miles in length and penetrating hundreds of miles into the interior, the territory occupied by the Americans presented a formidable land mass to be reconquered. "The prime objective of the war of 1775-1781, was the reduction of the colonial armies and the enforcement of the

authority of the crown," wrote Carrington. "The occupation of territory or cities by an inadequate force, while the opposing armies kept the field, was therefore of transient benefit." Much of the terrain was rugged and densely wooded, making it hard to conduct warfare in the traditional European manner. America's forests, hills, and swamps were better suited for military operations by irregulars, and guerilla fighters swarmed everywhere. In the end, two major geographical considerations proved to be too much for the British generals: the extent of the continent; and the great distance separating the American theater of war from Britain which made it hard to supply the army overseas.

Carrington's maps trace for us the course of the war in classical geographical-chronological fashion. The major campaigns, generally speaking, were concentrated in New England and Canada in 1775, and in the Middle Colonies during the years 1776 and 1777. From 1778 to 1781, however, the main military show shifted to the Southern theater of operations. Unfortunately, Carrington neglects to take note of one rather important sideshow — the campaigns of George Rogers Clark in the Old Northwest in 1778 and 1779.

Boston, around which the first campaign was waged, is the focus of two of Carrington's first four maps. Modern Boston is quite different in its outlines from the city Carrington pictures in 1775. At that time Boston was situated on a peninsula and joined to the mainland by an isthmus only fifty or sixty yards wide at its most narrow point. During May of 1775, the British army occupied Boston, and was ringed about by American forces which held the surrounding areas as well as the Massachusetts countryside. The army within the city and British fleet in the harbor could be threatened if American cannon were placed at two strategic locations: from the north at Charlestown on Bunker or Breed's Hill; and from the south on Dorchester Heights. Learning that the British commander intended to occupy Dorchester Heights, the Patriots decided upon an immediate countermove — they seized the high ground on the Charlestown peninsula. The American move precipitated the so-called battle of Bunker Hill on June 17, 1775. Although the British swept the Americans off the hill, they did so at a fearful cost. On March 4, 1776, the Americans occupied and fortified Dorchester Heights. Realizing they faced inevitable destruction, the British decided to evacuate Boston on March 17, 1776.

Canada was another focal point for the Patriots during the second half of 1775. Americans received word in June that the British were recruiting a force to invade New York. The Americans reacted with a plan for a two-pronged attack on Quebec. One prong, led by Benedict Arnold, left Cambridge in September and made its way through the Maine forests toward the objective. The second, commanded by General Richard Montgomery who replaced the ailing Philip Schuyler, left from Ticonderoga in August. After taking St. John and Montreal, this force marched along the St. Lawrence until it linked up with Arnold who lay before the walls of Quebec. In a blinding snowstorm on the last day of 1775, the combined forces launched an all-out assault. The attack ended in disaster and resulted in Montgomery's death. Although Arnold maintained a weak cordon around Quebec throughout the rest of the winter, the shattered remnants of the American army were forced to retreat all the way to Ticonderoga in the spring of 1776. Two of Carrington's maps cover these aspects of the Canadian campaign.

One of the greatest British blunders of the war was the decision to abandon efforts to reduce New England and to probe instead for weak spots in the other colonies where the spark of rebellion was supposedly weaker — in New York, New Jersey, Pennsylvania, and the South. During the summer of 1776, the British opened a campaign in New York with two objects in mind: the occupation of New York City; and the capture of Washington's army. Carrington has three maps dealing with these British efforts. When the campaign was over, General William Howe held New York City which became the main British base because of its strategic location and its superb deep-water harbor. But

Washington managed to save his army so that it could fight another day.

As the year 1776 was drawing to a close, the main American army fled in retreat across New Jersey with Howe in hot pursuit. Putting the Delaware River between him and the British, Washington withdrew into Pennsylvania and regrouped his forces. On Christmas Day, 1776, he recrossed the Delaware and delivered a brilliant stroke. Leading his men in a surprise attack on Trenton, Washington captured the Hessian garrison of more than 900 men. Returning to Pennsylvania with his prisoners, Washington recrossed the Delaware several days later to strike a second blow. Pinned up against the river by General Cornwallis, Washington slipped boldly past his opponent in the dark of night and smashed the British rear guard at Princeton on January 3, 1777. Carrington devotes three of his maps to these operations which helped to instil greater confidence in the Americans in their fighting ability.

The British in 1777 came forward with an ambitious plan for two campaigns that were designed to end the war. Along the northern front, they were to send two armies crashing down from Canada to invade New York. Their mission was to cut off New England from the rest of the colonies. The main army, under General John Burgoyne, was to push south from Canada down Lake Champlain until it reached the upper Hudson near Albany. A second force, commanded by Colonel Barry St. Leger, was to advance eastward from Oswego through the Mohawk River Valley until it also arrived at Albany. Along the southern front, there was to be a second campaign opened against Philadelphia, the American capital. General Howe, leaving from New York, was to capture the city. It was hoped that Howe would finish his offensive in time to return to New York and rush up the Hudson to assist Burgoyne near Albany.

The outcome of these two campaigns is covered in eleven of Carrington's maps. St. Leger, attacking from the west, was stopped and turned back in August. Burgoyne, pressing south toward Albany, met with success, at first, as he took Ticonderoga. But his western flank was exposed,

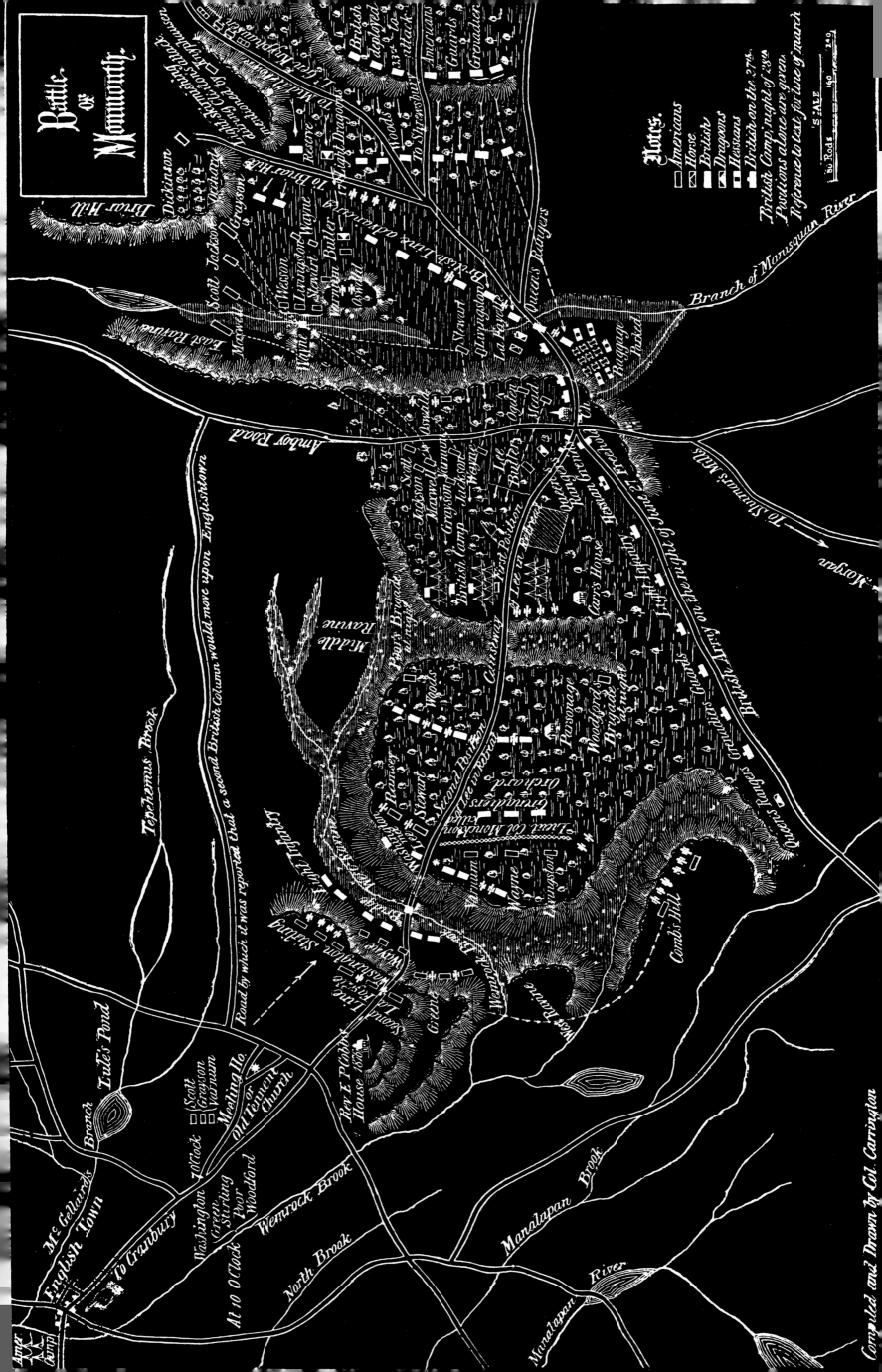

Siege of Newport

AUGUST 1778

American Commanders

SULLIVAN

GREENE, LIVINGSTON, HANCOCK, WEST, LAWSON, HENRY
VARNUM, GLOVER, LAFAYETTE

French Army and Fleet

COUNT D'ESTAING

British Commanders

PIGOT

HUYN, BANAU, DITFORTH, SEABOTH, PRESCOTT,
VOSBERG, SMITH, GREY, BOIT, FANNING

Strength, 6,000.

British Admirals
HOWE   BYRON

PLAN OF ATTACK.—The 10th of August was selected for the attack. The Americans were to cross from Tiverton, at Howland's Ferry, and the French were to land on the west side, opposite Byer's Island.

NOTE I.—Sullivan, without notice to the French Commander, crossed at Tiverton July 29th. The French fleet forced the west and middle passages on the eighth. A heavy storm scattered both French and British fleets, and Count D'Estaing did not regain port until the 20th. Between the 15th and 20th the Americans had established batteries from Parker's Hill across the island.

NOTE II.—The reported movement of Clinton from New York, with 4,000 troops led to a retreat, which began on the 26th of August. On the 29th the Americans still held Quaker Hill and Turkey Hill, as well as Butts' Hill. Livingston, Lawrence and Glover distinguished themselves in the defence, losing 67 men, and inflicting a loss of 248 upon their assailants.

NOTE III.—On the 30th one hundred vessels arrived in sight, with Clinton's division; but the retreat to the main land had been effected, under the personal supervision of Lafayette, "without leaving behind a single man, or the smallest article," as reported by Sullivan.

References :

CARRINGTON'S "BATTLES OF THE AMERICAN REVOLUTION," pp. 448-456.

School Histories :

Anderson, ¶ 75-6 ; p. 87.
Barnes, ¶ 2 ; p. 128.
Berard (Bush), ¶ 100; p. 165.
Goodrich, C.A.(Seaveys),¶ 36, p. 132.
Goodrich, S. G., ¶ 3-9; p. 242.
Hassard, ¶ 13-14 ; p. 200.

Holmes, ¶ 19 ; p. 134.
Lossing. ¶ 7 ; p. 163.
Quackenbos, ¶ 359 ; p. 259.
Ridpath, ¶ 8-10 ; p. 210-11.
Sadlier (Excel), ¶ 10 ; p. 199.
Stephens, A.H. ¶ 8-9; p. 207.

Swinton, ¶ 169-170 ; p. 139.
Scott, ¶ 11-14 ; p. 193-4.
Thalheimer (Eclectic), ¶ 273 ;
p. 155.
Venable, ¶ 147 ; p. 113.

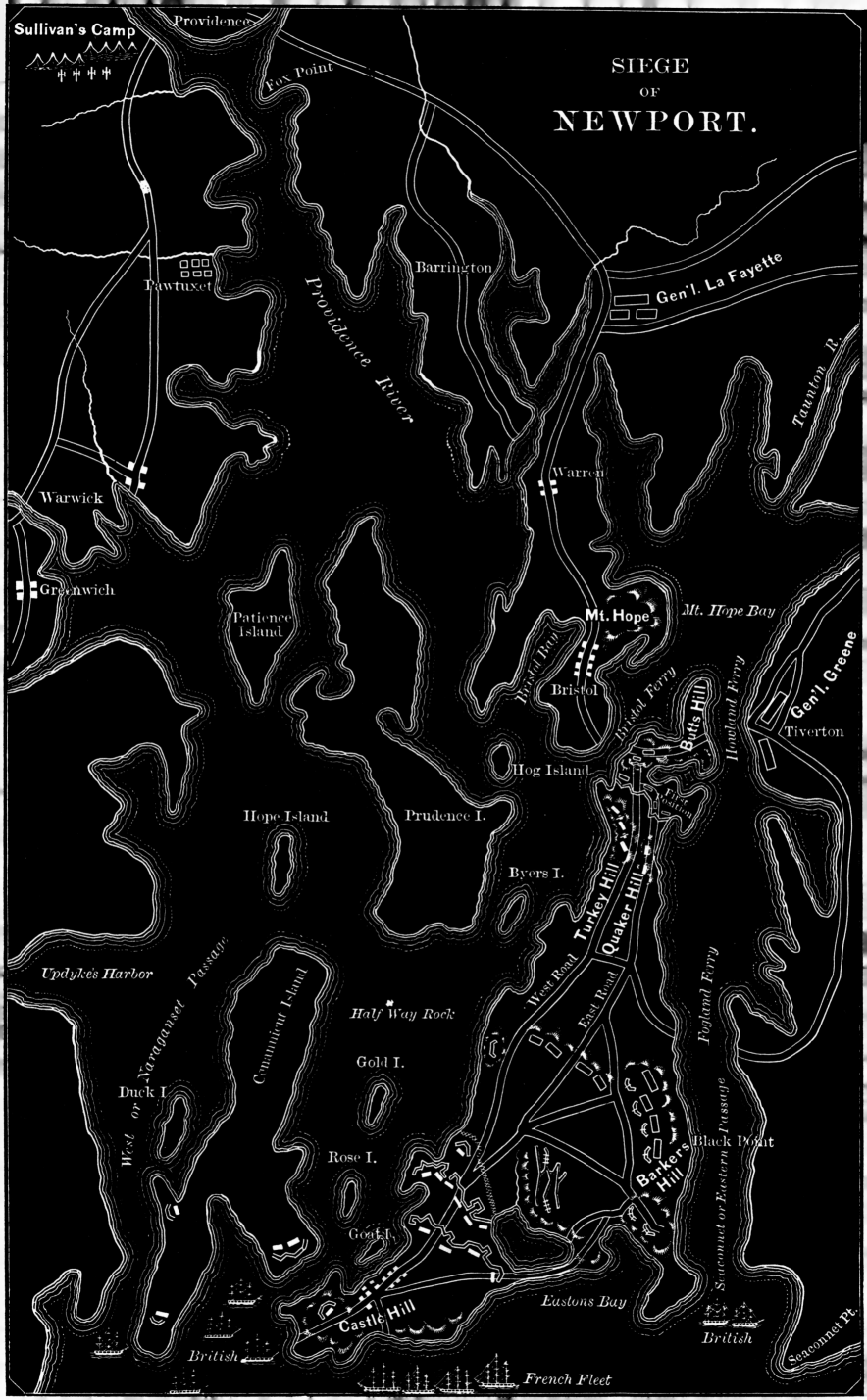

Siege of Savannah

SEPTEMBER 16th to OCTOBER 9th 1780

American Commanders
LINCOLN
LAURENS, McINTOSH, HUGER, DILLON, PULASKI

Strength, 3,600   Casualties, 457

French Commander
Lieut.-Gen. COUNT CHARLES HECTOR D'ESTAING

Strength, 6,000   Casualties, 651

POSITION OF THE ALLIED ARMIES.—The French fleet arrived off Tybee Island September 8th, and anchored near the bar. On the 9th the troops landed twelve miles below Savannah. and on the 16th D'Estaing summoned the garrison to surrender. General Prevost asked and gained a truce of twenty-four hours, during which interval Lt.-Col. Maitland skillfully eluded the American outposts, and joined, with eight hundred excellent troops. Surrender was then declined The American army joined the French on the 16th, and batteries were at once placed in position.

BRITISH POSITION.—At the first intimation that a large French fleet was off the coast, General Prevost removed the buoys from the harbor, and put a large force of negroes at work, to strengthen the post. New redoubts, made of double palmetto logs, interfilled with sand, a strong palisade, and a series of minor detached defences, were pushed forward with energy. Relays of men enabled the work to be carried on at night, as well as by day. Capt. Moncrieff, Engineer-in-charge, has left his notes, which are reproduced, on map. Major Graham made a sally Sept. 24, and Major McArthur another on the 27th, at night, but without valuable results.

NOTES.

NOTE I.—On the 5th of October, a battery of nine mortars, thirty-three heavy guns from the land side, and sixteen from the river, opened fire, and this was kept up until the 8th. Houses were burned, but little damage was done to the defences. It became evident that the siege would be protracted, and the season of the year was so dangerous that the French fleet could not remain longer on the coast. It was necessary to raise the siege, or storm the town.

NOTE II.—The force detailed for that assault consisted of 3,500 French troops; 600 American regulars; Pulaski's corps, and 250 militia; to form two columns.

NOTE III.—General Dillon, of the Irish Brigade, in the French service, was to take the extreme left, and attack the horse-shoe or sailor's battery, at the British right; D'Estaing and Lincoln were to attack Spring Hill, and Pulaski to attack a redoubt beyond, toward the direction of Dillon's advance, while Huger and Williams were to make feint attacks, upon the east side of town, and take advantage of any opportunity to force an entrance.

NOTE IV.—The batteries maintained fire, as if preparatory to an assault in front; but by the desertion of the Sergeant-Major of the Charleston Grenadiers, during the night, the enemy had knowledge of the real plan of attack.

NOTE V.—Dillon got involved in a marsh, and Huger could make little progress through the rice fields, and lost 27 men. Pulaski fell, mortally wounded, in a brave, but unsuccessful attack.

NOTE VI.—The main column, which was also accompanied by Laurens and McIntosh, forced the palisades and the ditch, but were met by the British Grenadiers and Glazier's Marines, whose concentrated fire, for fifty-five minutes, was too heavy to be silenced. Sergeant Jasper received his death wound here. Bush and Holmes, 2d S. C. Regt., planted their colors within the redoubt, and fell in their defence.

NOTE VII.—D'Estaing was twice wounded. The French lost 15 officers killed and 43 wounded; rank and file, 168 killed and 411 wounded.

NOTE VIII.—The siege of Savannah was at an end. Prompt attack, when the troops landed, would have promised success.

References :

CARRINGTON'S "BATTLES OF THE AMERICAN REVOLUTION," pp. 476-483.

School Histories :

Anderson, ¶ 88 ; p. 90.
Barnes, ¶ 2 ; p. 129.
Berard (Bush), ¶ 105-6 ; p. 166-7.
Goodrich, C. A.(Seaveys) ¶ 4 ; p. 134.
Goodrich, S. G., ¶ 1-6 ; p. 250.
Hassard, ¶ 6 ; p. 204.

Holmes, ¶ 10 ; p. 141.
Lossing, ¶ 11 ; p. 170-1.
Quackenbos, ¶ 369 ; p. 267.
Ridpath, ¶ 9-10 ; p. 215.
Sadlier (Excel.), ¶ 14 ; p. 200-1.
Stephens, A. H., ¶ 23 ; p. 212.

Swinton, ¶ 184-7 ; p. 141.
Scott, ¶ 1-3 ; p. 196-7.
Thalheimer (Eclectic), ¶ 285 ; p. 163.
Venable, ¶ 155 ; p. 118.

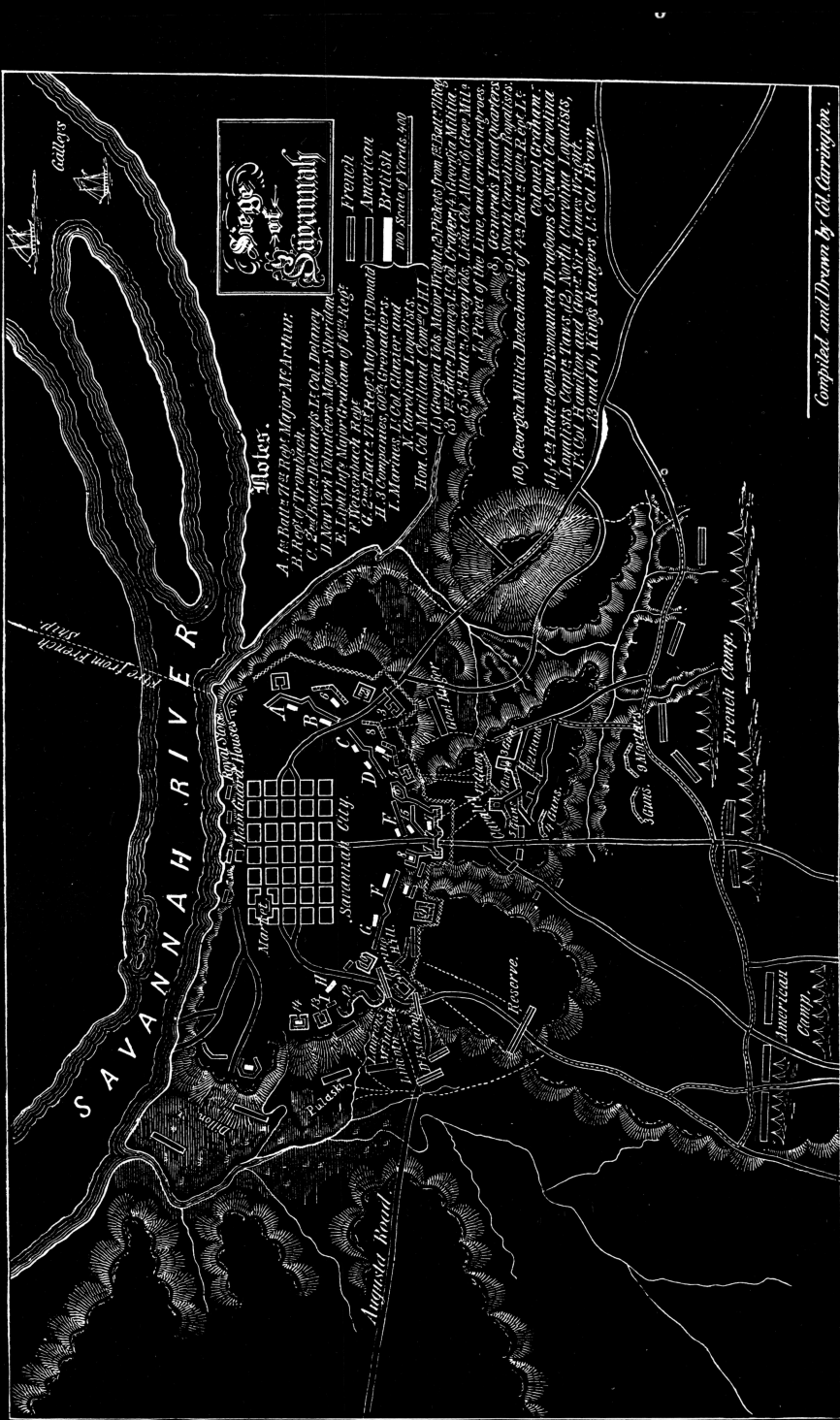

Siege of Savannah

Compiled and Drawn by Col. Carrington.

French
American
British

100 Scale of Yards. 400

Notes.

A. 1st Batt. 71st Reg.t Major M.cArthur.
B. Reg.t of Tromback.
C. 2.d Batt. Delaneys Lt Col. Delancey.
D. New York Volunteers. Major Sheridan.
E. Light Inf.y Major Graham of 16.th Reg.t
F. Weissenbach Reg.t
G. 2.d Batt. 71st Reg.t Major M.cDonald.
H. 3 Companies 60.th Grenadiers.
I. Marines L.t Col Glazier. and
   N. Carolina Loyalists.
Hon. Col. Maitland Com.r C.H.I
(1) Georgia 16.t Major Wright. (2) Pickets from 2.d Batt. They
(3) Ft Batt. Delancys Lt Col. Cruger. 4. Georgia Militia
(5) 3.d Batt. Jersey Vols. Lieut Col Allen. 6 Heer Mila
(7) Picket of the Line. and armed negroes.
(8) General's Head Quarters.
(9) South Carolina Royalists.
Colonel Graham.
(10) Georgia Militia. Detachment of 4.th Batt. 60.th Reg.t L.t
(11) 4.th Batt. 60.th Dismounted Dragoons C.South Carolina
Loyalists. Capt.s Tows. 12. North Carolina Loyalists.
L.t Col. Hamilton and Geo.r Sir. Jn.o Wright.
13 and 14. Kings Rangers L.t Col. Brown.

Siege of Charleston

MAY 12th, 1780

American Commanders

WHIPPLE   LINCOLN   WOODFORD

Strength, 3,000.   Casualties, 276.

MEM. *The schedule of prisoners, which was made up by Major Andre, embraced the names of all male citizens. Total, 5,618.*

AMERICAN POSITION. The garrison embraced 2,200 regulars, and about 1,000 militia, when Clinton crossed the Ashley; but his delay, for Patterson to join him from Savannah allowed Woodford to steal quietly into the city April 7th, with 700 Virginia troops. They had made a march of 500 miles in 30 days. Commodore Whipple withdrew his ships behind a boom, and they rendered no service. Their guns were mounted in the city. He over-estimated the resisting capacity of Fort Moultrie.

British Commander

CLINTON

Strength, 8,500.   Casualties, 265.

BRITISH POSITION. Clinton left New York, Dec. 26th, but storms dispersed his fleet. All the cavalry and most of the artillery horses perished. Tybee Island, near Savannah, was the first rendezvous; but it was not until February 11th, that the troops landed on St. John's Island, thirty miles below Charleston.

They were transferred to James Island, crossed Stono and Ashley rivers, and established themselves across the narrow neck above Charleston on the 12th of March.

NOTES.

NOTE I.—Admiral Arbuthnot weighed anchor March 9th, leading with the Roebuck frigate, and passed Fort Moultrie with a loss of but 27 men. On the 20th he crossed the bar, and on the 29th he landed a brigade of 500 seamen and marines at Mount Pleasant. This compelled the Americans to abandon their outpost at L'Empries Point. On the 4th of May 200 seamen and marines landed on Sullivan Island, and Fort Moultrie was surrendered.

NOTE II.—The British broke ground on the night of April 1st, at 800 yards before the American lines, and on the 10th demanded surrender of the city. April 19th the second parallel was opened at 450 yards, and on the 6th of May, the third parallel was established by converting a canal into a dry ditch.

NOTE III.—The Americans lost by the surrender, 405 pieces of ordnance of various calibre.

NOTE IV.—The map also indicates the position of Admiral Parker's fleet, June 28th, 1776, when Clinton made his first attempt to capture Charleston, and the resistance at Fort Moultrie, endorsed by Governor Rutledge, but opposed by General Charles Lee, defeated the British attempt to capture Charleston.

References:

CARRINGTON'S "BATTLES OF THE AMERICAN REVOLUTION," pp. 492-498.

School Histories:

Anderson, ¶ 89-90 ; p. 91.
Barnes, ¶ 1 ; p. 132-3.
Berard (Bush), ¶ 115; p. 169.
Goodrich, C.A. (Seaveys), ¶ 13, p. 137.
Goodrich, S. G., ¶ 5-6; p. 262.
Hassard, ¶ 1-3 ; p. 209-10.

Holmes, ¶ 11 ; p. 142.
Lossing, ¶ 1-6; p. 174-5.
Quackenbos, ¶ 371 ; p. 269.
Ridpath, ¶ 2-3 ; p. 216-17.
Sadlier (Excel), ¶ 15 ; p. 201.
Stephens, A.H. ¶ 1-4; p. 214-15.

Swinton, ¶ 193-5 ; p. 144.
Scott, ¶ 3-5 ; p. 201-2.
Thalheimer (Eclectic), ¶ 285 ; p. 163.
Venable, ¶ 158 ; p. 110

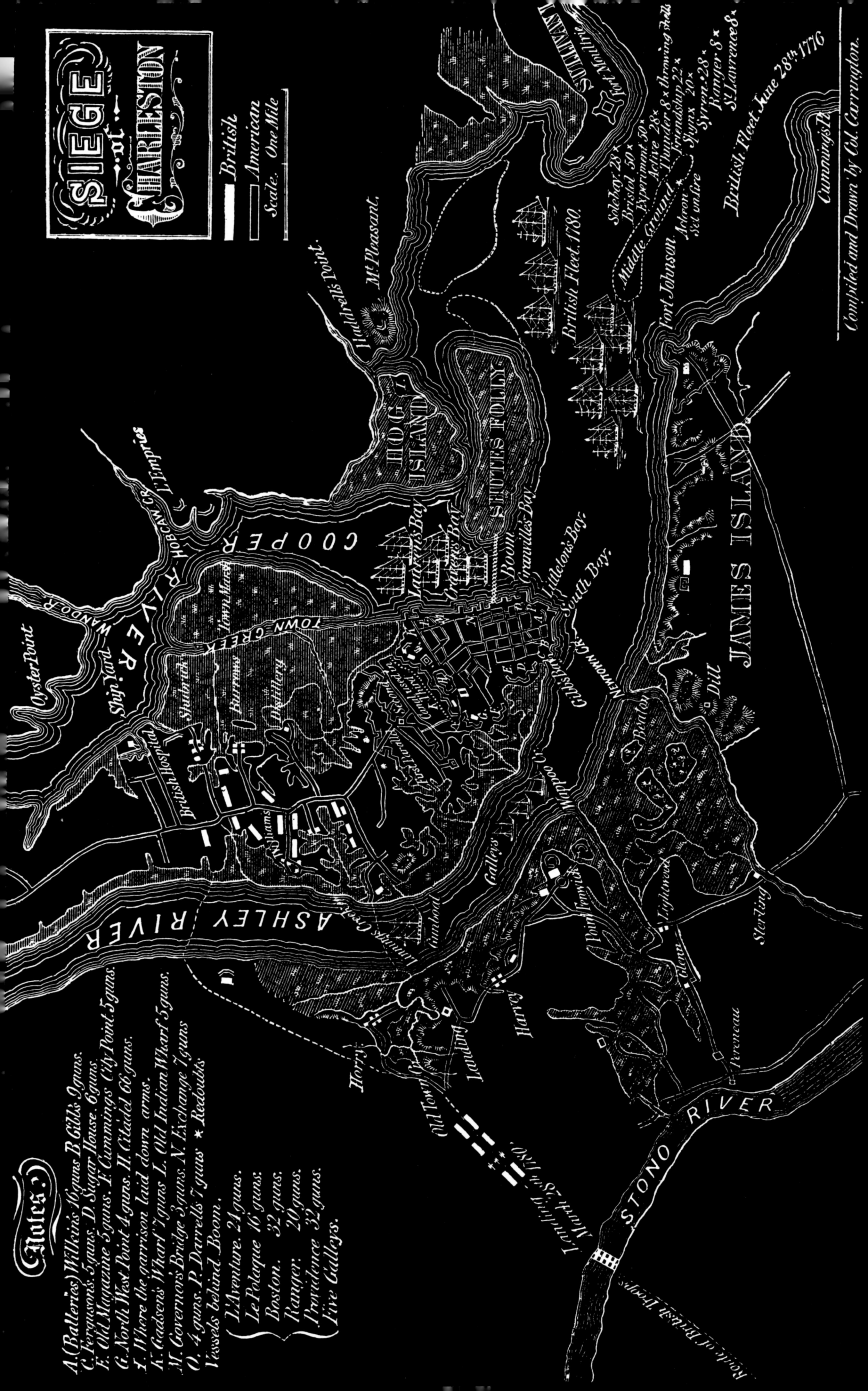

Battle of Springfield

AND

Operations from Staten Island

DURING JUNE, 1780

American Commanders	British Commanders
GREENE	CLINTON KNYPHAUSEN
Maxwell, Stark, Angell, Jackson, Lee	Sterling, Matthews, Simcoe, Stirn, Tryon
Webb, Dickinson, Dayton, Shreve	
Estimated Strength Available 7,800	Strength, 5,000

AMERICAN POSITION. Washington held firm hold of his well protected camp near Morristown, carefully guarded the pass at Chatham, and so disposed his advance posts as to be fully advised of British activity. (*A reference to map 11, p. 26-7, will indicate the relations of Staten Island to the operations referred to*).

BRITISH MOVEMENTS. Lieut. Gen. Knyphausen, commanding at New York, during Clinton's operations against Charleston, determined to draw Washington into a general engagement and seize his camp. On the 6th of June, with Matthews, Tryon, Sterling, and 5,000 excellent troops, he crossed from Staten Island, by a bridge of boats, to Elizabethtown Point.

The mutinous conduct of the American army, after a winter of great severity, and the suffering incident to scant food, clothing, fuel, medicines and all necessaries, had inspired the opinion that a prompt invasion would induce many to return to British allegiance.

Sterling advanced toward Elizabethtown at daylight, but the militia were on the alert. He was mortally wounded by an American sentry, and Knyphausen took his place at the front. When the sun had risen, the British army not only discovered that orchards, houses and single trees were sheltering keen marksmen, but that the regiment of Col. Elias Dayton was rapidly forming to resist their march. The Queen's Rangers (Simcoe's) led the Hessian column; but instead of any friendly indications, there was opposition at every step. Connecticut Farms, seven miles beyond Elizabethtown, was burned, with its church and parsonage, and the wife of Chaplain Caldwell was killed by a bullet.

When within half a mile of Springfield, it was found, that, as Dayton fell back, he was amply supported by Maxwell on the bank of the Rahway, and that Washington was fully prepared for the issue.

A stormy night, enlivened by watch fires, which blazed on every hill, warned Knyphausen that he was surrounded by vigilant adversaries, and he retired to Staten Island.

Clinton, returning from Charleston, reached Staten Island on the 17th of June, and he also resolved to strike the camp and magazines of Washington, at Morristown. Troops were embarked, ostensibly, to ascend the Hudson and attack West Point. Washington left Greene to command, behind Springfield, with Maxwell, Stark and Col. Lee, and marched on the 22d eleven miles toward the Hudson; but upon appreciating the *feint* of Clinton, regained his post.

The Battle of Springfield followed

NOTE I.—The British advanced in two columns, at 5 o'clock A. M. June 23d, with 5,000 infantry, cavalry and 18 guns ; one column (Clinton's), by the Connecticut Farms' Road, and the other (Knyphausen's), by the Vauxhall road.

NOTE II.—At the first bridge over the Rahway, Clinton found that Col. Angell, with a Rhode Island regiment and one gun, occupied an orchard on a hill, and practically commanded the bridge. He at once gained high ground for his own guns, but finding their effect to be inconsiderable, forded the stream ; turned Angell's position and forced him back to the second bridge, where Colonel Shreve disputed the advance. This officer lost one-fourth of his men; but found himself promptly supported by the brigades of Maxwell and Stark. They took a position at a mill which afforded strength, and Greene so disposed of Dickinson's militia as to check the British ardor.

NOTE III.—Knyphausen's column attempted to seize the Chatham pass, in the rear, and thus gain the avenue to the Morristown camp. At Little's bridge, on the Vauxhall road, he was met by Lee's cavalry, well supported by Col. Ogden's regiment, and a brisk struggle took place for its possession. Greene promptly moved the regiments of Webb and Jackson, with one gun, to the Chatham pass, and the object of the expedition was foiled.

NOTE IV.—Clinton burned Springfield, returned to Staten Island, removed his bridge of boats, and the last New Jersey campaign closed.

NOTE V.—The American militia made no return of their losses. The regular troops had 13 killed and 61 wounded. The British loss was not officially stated, but was estimated at 150, including missing.

References:

CARRINGTON'S "BATTLES OF THE AMERICAN REVOLUTION," pp. 498-502.

School Histories:

Anderson, ¶ —; p. 102.
Barnes, ¶ —; p. —.
Berard (Bush), ¶ 123; p. 174.
Goodrich, C. A. (Seaveys), ¶ —; p. —.
Goodrich, S. G., ¶ 5, p. 265.
Hassard, ¶ 2; p. 214.

Holmes, ¶ —; p. —.
Lossing, ¶ 13; p. 178-9.
Quackenbos, ¶ —; p. —.
Ridpath, ¶ —; p. —.
Sadlier, (Excel), ¶ —; p. —.
Stephens, A. H. ¶ —; p. —.

Swinton, ¶ —; p. —.
Scott, ¶ 11 ; p. 205.
Thalheimer (Eclectic), ¶ —, p. —;
Venable, ¶ —; p. —.

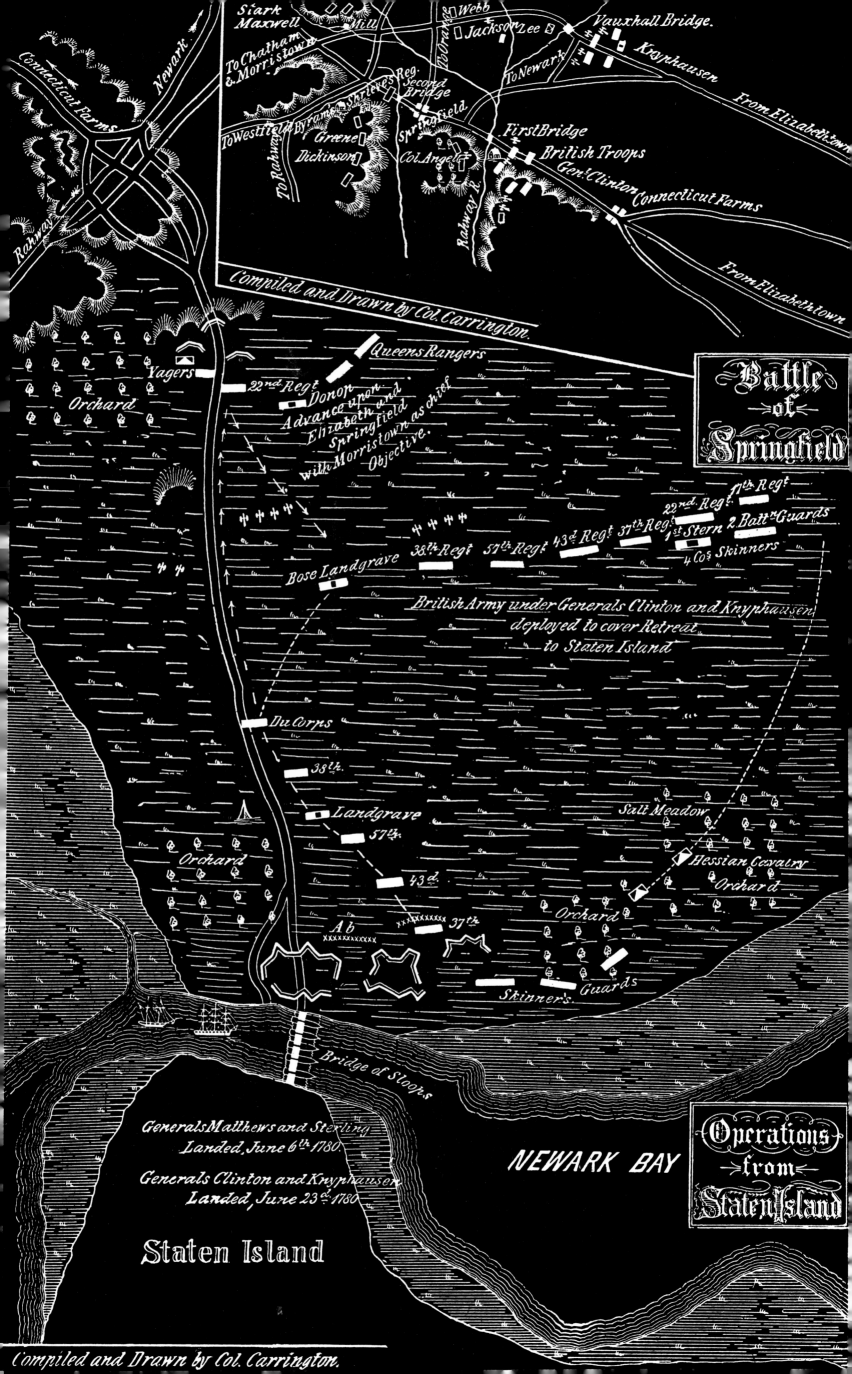

Outline Map

OF THE

→ Hudson River ←

FROM

Dobbs Ferry to Fishkill and Newburgh

INCLUDING

Tappan and Tarrytown

HAVERSTRAW, where Andre landed, from British Sloop, Vulture;

PEEKSKILL, NORTH CASTLE & WHITE PLAINS

ALSO

Stony Point

FORT INDEPENDENCE

FORT CLINTON   FORT MONTGOMERY

FORT PUTNAM and WEST POINT

NOTE.—**Stony Point** is memorable, as follows:

It was **stormed under direction of Washington**, by Wayne, Febiger, Webb, Meigs, Butler, Lee, Muhlenburg, Fleury, Knox, and Gibbon. July 16, 1779. (*Carrington's "Battles," pp. 472-474*).

It was **abandoned** (same, p. 474).

It was **re-occupied by Clinton**; but **abandoned** (Oct. 25, 1779). *Carrington's "Battles," p. 476.*

MEM. *As the Hudson River separated New England from the central colonies, and its control was contended for, by both armies, it is to be noted, that Governor Tryon, both in 1777 and 1779, made incursions into Connecticut, in vain attempting to divert Washington from his general plans. April 25, 1777, when Fairfield and Danbury were visited, he was bravely resisted by Arnold, at Ridgefield. General David Wooster was fatally wounded. July 4, 1779, Tryon visited New Haven, and on the 8th and 9th burned Fairfield, including 2 churches, 83 houses and shops, 2 school-houses, jail and County-House.*

British expeditions, out of New York, into Westchester County, were frequent.

Battle of Camden or Sander's Creek

AUGUST 16th, 1780

American Commanders
GATES

Porterfield, Armstrong, Williams, Gist, DeKalb, Caswell, Singleton, Stevens, Marquis Armand, Rutherford, Gregory

Strength, 3,052   Casualties, 971, beside missing

British Commanders
CORNWALLIS

Rawdon, Tarleton, Webster, Hamilton, Bryan,   McLeod

Strength, 2,239   Casualties, 324

AMERICAN MOVEMENTS.—The army of Gates, strengthened by that of DeKalb, left Hillsborough, N. C., July 27th, crossed Deep River at Buffalo Ford, and by the 3d of August, 1780, gained the Peedee River, and united with Porterfield's command. On the 7th, the North Carolina militia, under Caswell, joined, and on the 13th, Gates encamped at Rugely's Mills, twelve miles above Camden. On the 14th, Stevens joined, with 700 Virginia militia. The troops of De Kalb, 1,400 men, Maryland and Delaware troops, accompanied him from Morristown, New Jersey, having left headquarters, April 16th.

On the 15th of August, Gates ordered the army to march, at ten o'clock that night, to attack Camden, and insisted upon the order, after Adjutant-General Williams exhibited the daily Returns, showing that the real force was less than half his estimate. He did not know that Cornwallis had joined Rawdon at Camden.

Marquis Armand, with his squadron of 60 dragoons, led the advance, in spite of his protest against using mounted men for pioneer night service, as it required perfect silence. Porterfield and Armstrong were to take the woods, on his flank, and give him full support.

BRITISH MOVEMENTS.—Cornwallis, advised of Gates' force and his advance, alike intended to surprise his enemy. Upon reaching Sander's Creek, five miles from Camden, between two and three o'clock in the morning, the advance guard of 40 cavalry, and mounted infantry, met and routed Armand's detachment. Porterfield was mortally wounded in giving his support, and both armies waited for the break of day for further developments.

NOTE I—The American *first line* was formed as follows: Right Wing, under General Gist, with the Delaware troops of DeKalb; Centre, under General Caswell, with North Carolina militia; Left Wing, under General Stevens, with raw Virginia militia. Singleton's guns occupied the road. General Smallwood commanded the *second line* with the First Maryland brigade.

NOTE II.—The British *first line* was as follows: Right Wing, Webster, with 23d and 33d regiments, and three companies of light infantry. Lord Rawdon commanded the left wing, viz.: Volunteers of Ireland, the Legion Infantry, Hamilton's Corps, and Bryan's Refugees, and five guns under McLeod. The two battalions of the 71st regiment, with two guns, formed the second line. Tarleton's dragoons remained in column, on account of the thickness of the wood, to act as required.

NOTE III.—Upon crossing Sander's Creek, the British army entered upon a narrow belt of land, bordered on each side by an impassable swamp, while the American line, also between the swamps, on a widening area, would become exposed to any flank movement, unless they firmly held their original ground.

NOTE IV.—Before the action, Gates had learned from a prisoner, taken in the night skirmish, that Cornwallis was in command; but hesitated so long as to what was to be done, that he lost the opportunity for retreat to Rugely's Mills. Stevens pronounced it to be anything but right, and in the silence of Gates as to orders, gallantly followed the suggestion of Adjutant-General Williams, to attack the British right wing as it advanced, before it could gain room for full deployment. Skirmishers were ordered to take single trees for cover, and aid the movement.

NOTE V—"It was calm and hazy, so that the smoke settled, until it was difficult," says Cornwallis, "to see the effect of a heavy and well-directed fire on both sides." He observed a movement on the American left, which he supposed to indicate some change in their order of battle. He at once precipitated Webster's regiments upon the Virginia militia, before they could gain the position they sought. They threw down their loaded arms, and fled. The North Carolina militia, except a small force under Gregory, also fled.

NOTE VI.—The British right wing, having then broken through, next attacked the 1st Maryland brigade, where it met firm resistance, until Tarleton's dragoons came to their support, when, overwhelmed with numbers, they retired.

NOTE VII.—The British left wing was firmly received by DeKalb. He bore down upon them with the bayonet, broke through their ranks, wheeled to the left, and fought, until his force was enveloped by the British right wing, which turned back to charge this, suddenly, adverse tide of battle. DeKalb fell, wounded in five places, still confident that victory was certainly with the Americans.

NOTE VIII.—The rout of the militia was utter. Gates hurried to Charlotteville, sixty miles, and by the 20th, reached Hillsborough, one hundred and eighty miles from Camden, without fugitives sufficient for an escort. The Delaware regiment was almost destroyed, while the Maryland troops lost more than 300 in killed, wounded, and prisoners. Forty-one officers were killed or wounded.

NOTE IX.—The gallantry of DeKalb's conduct is shown by the British casualties, which Cornwallis admitted to be 324.

NOTE X.—Of the missing from the Maryland division, it is to be noted, to their credit, that by the 29th, 700 had rejoined the army.

NOTE XI.—The British captured 7 guns, 1,000 prisoners, 2,000 muskets, and all the baggage of the American army.

References :

CARRINGTON'S "BATTLES OF THE AMERICAN REVOLUTION," pp. 513-523.

School Histories:

Anderson, ¶ 93 ; p. 92.
Barnes, ¶ 2 ; p. 133.
Berard (Bush), ¶ 119; p. 170.
Goodrich, C. A.(Seaveys) ¶ 15; p. 138.
Goodrich, S. G., ¶ 4-8; p. 264.
Hassard, ¶ 8 ; p. 212.

Holmes, ¶ 13 ; p. 143.
Lossing, ¶ 9 ; p. 177.
Quackenbos, ¶ 277 ; p. 274-5.
Ridpath, ¶ 7 ; p. 218.
Sadlier (Excel.), ¶ 17; p. 201-2.
Stephens, A. H., ¶ 6-7 ; p. 217.

Swinton, ¶ 4 ; p. 157.
Scott, ¶ 7 ; p. 203.
Thalheimer (Eclectic), ¶ 288 ; p. 165.
Venable, ¶ 161 ; p. 121.

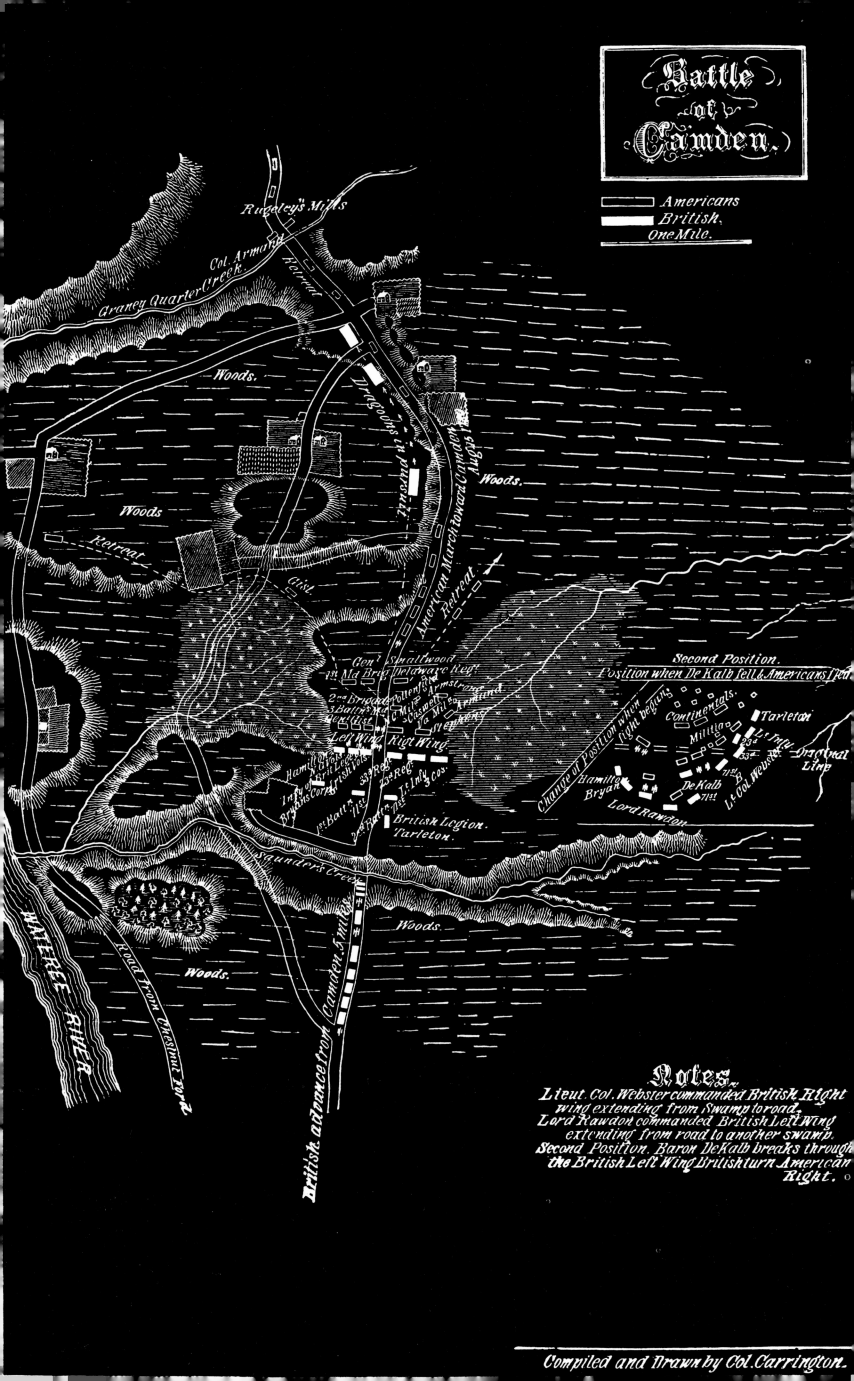

Arnold at Petersburg

APRIL 25th, 1781

NOTES.—Benedict Arnold, having a force of 1,553 men, sailed to City Point (see map page), and on the 25th marched to Petersburg, arriving at 10 o'clock. Generals Steuben and Muhlenberg were at the post with about 1,000 militia. They advanced to a strong position before Brandon (Bradford) which compelled the Queen's Rangers and Rifles to make a long detour to cut off their retreat and gain Petersburg. Steuben fell back to cover Petersburg; but being unable to meet the opposing superior force, in action, recrossed the Appomattox River, with a loss of only twenty men. A third position was taken on Baker's Hill, which Arnold did not venture to assail.

Arnold claims that " he did not pursue because the enemy took up the bridge," and that he destroyed four thousand hogsheads of tobacco, one ship and a number of small vessels on the stocks and in the river.

References:

CARRINGTON'S " BATTLES OF THE AMERICAN REVOLUTION," pp. 589–590.

Arnold at Richmond

JANUARY 5th, 1780

NOTES.—BENEDICT ARNOLD, appointed Brigadier General in the British army, as pay for treason, left New York December 19, 1780, with sixteen hundred men for Virginia. Lieut. Col. Simcoe (Queen's Rangers), and Lieut. Col. Dundas, 18th Regiment (Scotch), belonged to his command.

A gale separated the ships; but on the 31st he transferred 1,200 men to small vessels and moved up James River. On the 3d of January, at night, Simcoe landed at Hood's Point, to spike a small battery, and on the 4th the expedition landed at Westover, nearly twenty-five miles below Richmond, and marched immediately to that city.

On the 5th, Arnold entered Richmond; Simcoe dislodged a small force of two hundred militia which Col. John Nichols had assembled on Richmond Hill; and some mounted men on Shoer's Hill quickly retired. A foundry, laboratory and some shops were burned at Westham, nearly seven miles above Richmond, as well as some public records which had been taken there for safety. A proposition sent to Governor Jefferson, dictating terms upon which the buildings might be saved, for the privilege of quietly taking away the tobacco, was rejected; and, burning as many houses as time permitted, Arnold retired without loss.

Five brass guns, three hundred stand of arms found in the loft of the capitol, and in a wagon, with a few quartermaster's stores, constituted the chief articles of capture.

References:

CARRINGTON'S " BATTLES OF THE AMERICAN REVOLUTION," pp. 548-9

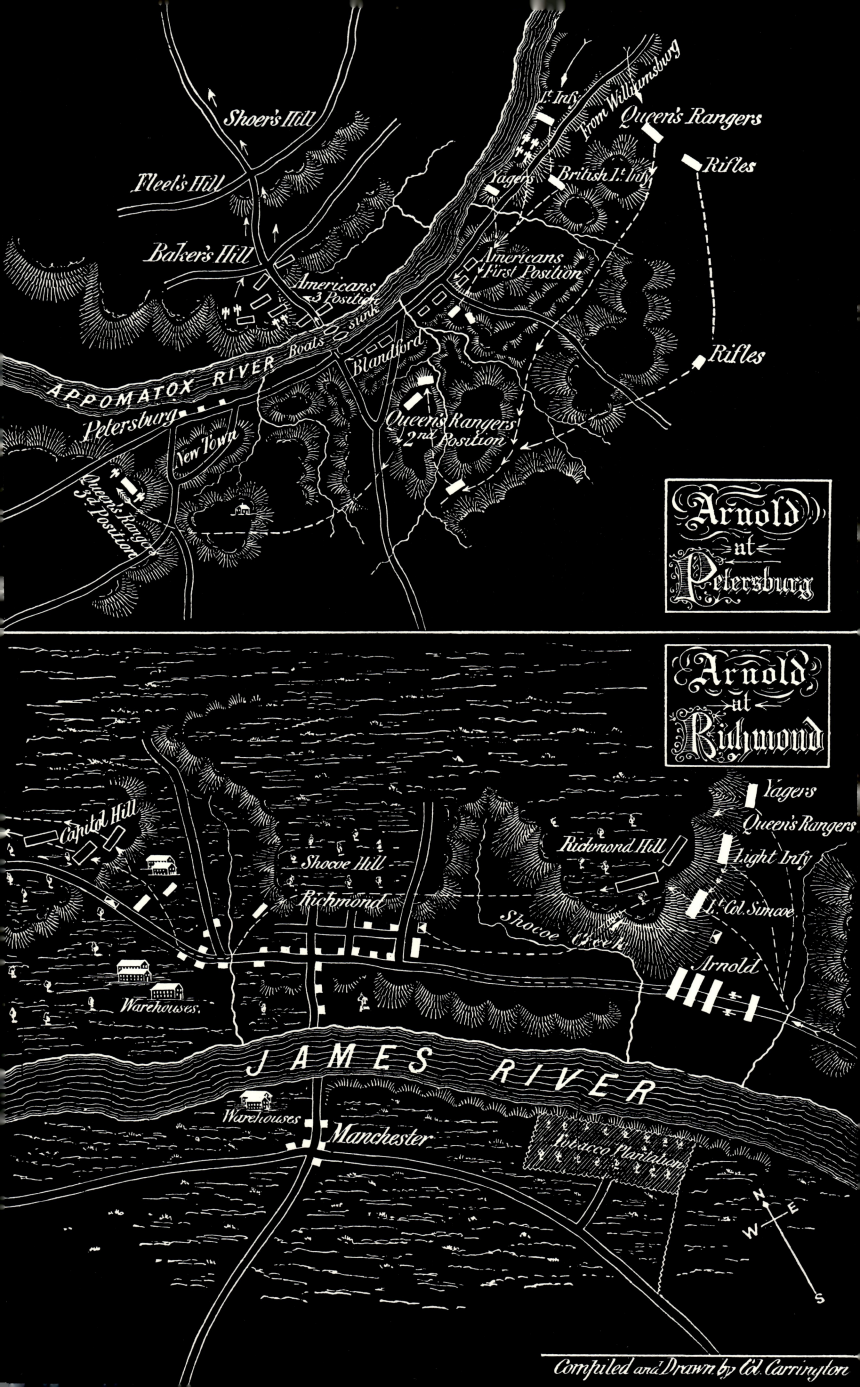

➤ Battle of Cowpens ◄

JANUARY 7th, 1781

American Commanders

MORGAN

**COL. WASHINGTON.   HOWARD.   McDOWELL.   PICKENS.
CUNNINGHAM.   BEATTY.   TRIPLETT.   McCALL.**

Strength, 1,250   Casualties, 72.

AMERICAN FORMATION. The battle was fought near Broad River, about two miles south of the North Carolina boundary line, on ground used for pasture, and familiarly known as Cow Pens. Broad River wound around Morgan's left, and was parallel with his rear, and the position was selected by him, to prevent retreat and compel his men to fight. An open woodland sloped to the front, which Tarleton said " could be no better for mounted men."

Morgan occupied the summit with the regular troops. Beatty's Georgians, 150 men, held the right, Triplett's and Tate's Virginians held the centre. The Maryland battalion, 300 men, held the left. Lieut. Col. Howard commanded this line. Pickens held a line of 270 men, in open order, about 150 yards in advance of the hill, while Major Cunningham, of Georgia, and Major McDowell, of South Carolina, were posted at an equal farther advance, with 150 picked sharp-shooters, under orders to take the cover of trees, fire only at short range, and fall back, firing, as they could still find cover.

Pickens was ordered to reserve fire until the enemy came within fifty yards, and after two volleys, to retire to the left of the regulars; but, if charged by cavalry, only one man in three must take part in the volley, while the rest should reserve their fire until the actual charge, or the troopers should turn back.

The regulars were advised of these orders, and instructed, if they were forced from their first position, to re-form on the next hill, and be prepared to face about and renew the attack. Col. Washington's cavalry and Col. McCall's mounted men were out of sight, in the rear of the hill.

BRITISH FORMATION. Tarleton made his advance at seven o'clock in the morning, with force well worn from hard marching, but under advices that a large force of militia was on the way to join Morgan. Dragoons on each flank, and in rear, supported the infantry, as designated on the map, and two guns opened fire from the intervals between battalions. The 71st Regiment formed, slightly in the rear, as a reserve.

NOTE I.—The sharp-shooters closely obeyed orders, and finally retreated around the American left for re-formation in the rear and to the right. One detachment of dragoons pursued them, as if they were fugitives.

NOTE II.—The British guns are moved to the front, but the resistance of the main line is so obstinate that, Tarleton, with the 71st and two hundred dragoons, takes part in the charge. Howard throws back his right wing, and this is at first taken for an order to retreat. Morgan promptly orders the troops to face about, deliver fire, and charge with the bayonet. The British were within thirty yards.

NOTE III.—Meanwhile the American cavalry move around by the left of the hill and attack the flank and rear of the troops which had pursued the retiring militia. The latter gain their assigned position, and are already ascending the hill to assist Morgan. (See map).

NOTE IV.—Nearly every British gunner had been killed or wounded at his gun. Pickens' militia attack the 71st Regiment by the flank, as they ascend the hill, and the whole force is at the mercy of the cross-fire of the American detachments

NOTE V.—Tarleton escaped with forty troopers; received a sword cut from Washington, who was also wounded in the knee, and the rest of the command surrendered.

NOTE VI.—Two standards, thirty-five wagons, one hundred horses, eight hundred muskets, two cannon and six hundred prisoners, were trophies of the action.
The British lost in killed and wounded, 129 officers and men.

References :

CARRINGTON'S "BATTLES OF THE AMERICAN REVOLUTION," pp. 540-547.

School Histories :

Anderson, ¶ 104 ; p. 95.
Barnes, ¶ 1 ; p. 137.
Berard (Bush), ¶ 129 ; p. 173.
Goodrich, C. A. (Seaveys), ¶ 24 ; p. 141.
Goodrich, S. G., ¶ 4-5 ; p. 272.
Hassard, ¶ 10 ; p. 219-20.

Holmes, ¶ 6 ; p. 153.
Lossing, ¶ 4 ; p. 182.
Quackenbos, ¶ 388 ; p. 284-5.
Ridpath, ¶ 6 ; p. 223.
Sadlier, (Excel), ¶ 18 ; p. 203.
Stephens, A. H. ¶ 6-7 ; p. 223-4.

Swinton, ¶ 7 ; p. 158.
Scott, ¶ 5 ; p. 210-11.
Thalheimer (Eclectic), ¶ 289, p. 165 ;
Venable, ¶ 166 ; p. 165.

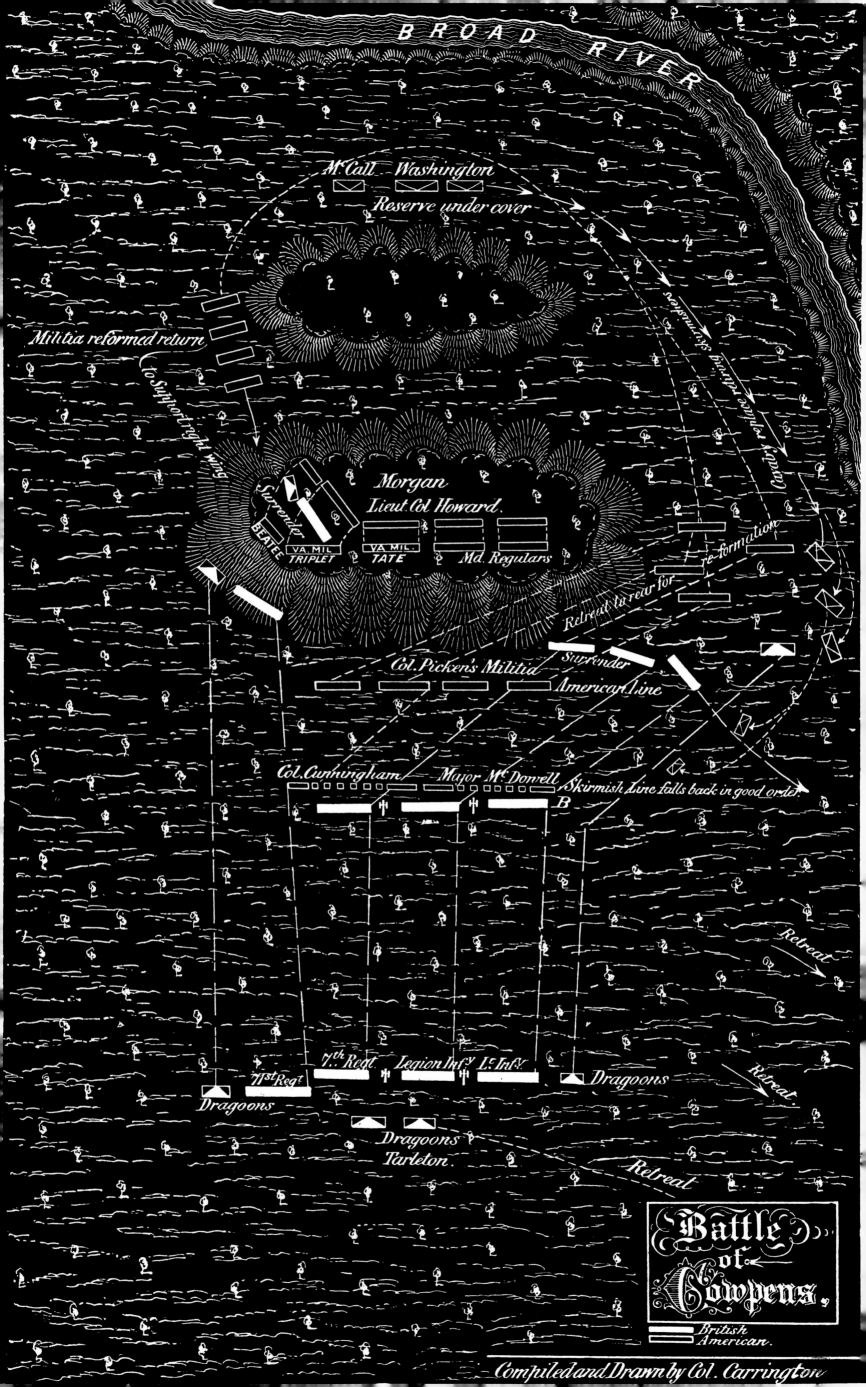

BROAD RIVER

McCall   Washington

Reserve under cover

Militia reformed return

to support right wing

Surrender
BEATEE

Morgan
Lieut Col Howard.

VA. MIL.
TRIPLET

VA. MIL.
TATE

Md. Regulars

Cavalry return charge

re-formation

Retreat to rear for

Surrender

American Line

Col. Picken's Militia

Col. Cunningham   Major McDowell

Skirmish Line falls back in good order.

B

Retreat.

Retreat.

7th Regt.   Legion Infy   Lt Infy

71st Regt.

Dragoons

Dragoons

Dragoons
Tarleton.

Retreat.

Battle
of
Cowpens.

British
American.

Compiled and Drawn by Col. Carrington

Operations in Southern States

Battles

References :—"Carrington's Battles of the American Revolution."

		PAGE.
Brier Creek	**Mar. 3, 1779**	464
Camden	**Aug. 16, 1780**	513
King's Mountain	Oct. 7, 1780	520
Blackstock	Nov. 20, 1780	522
Cowpens	Jan. 17, 1781	542
Guilford Court House	Mar. 15, 1781	556
Hobkirk's Hill	**Apr. 25, 1781**	571
Eutaw Springs	Sept. 8, 1781	578
Jamestown	**July 9, 1781**	607

Sieges

		PAGE.
Savannah	**by American and French troops**	477
Charleston	**by British troops**	496
Augusta	by American troops	520
Ninety Six	by American troops	574
Yorktown	by American and French troops	631

Minor Operations

		PAGE.
Moore's Creek Bridge, Va.	Dec. 9, 1775	174
Quinton's Bridge, Va.	Mar. 18, 1778	405
Tatnal's Plantation, S. C.	Nov. 27, 1778 (Savannah taken)	460
Beaufort, S. C.	**Feb. 3, 1779** (A sharp action)	464
Kettle Creek, Ga.	Feb. 14, 1779 (Tories routed by Pickens and Dooley)	464
Stono Ferry, S. C.	Apr. 20, 1779	465
Waxhaw Creek, S. C.	May 29, 1780 (no quarter given)	497
Ramseur's Mills, S. C.	June 20, 1780 (sharp action)	498
Williamson's Plantation, S. C.	July 12, 1780	507
Rocky Mount, S. C.	July 30, 1780 (a bold assault)	507
Rocky Mount, S. C.	**Aug. 1, 1780** (skirmish)	507
Hanging Rock, S. C.	**Aug. 6, 1780** (a formal action)	508
NOTE.—*Andrew Jackson, afterward President, was a drummer-boy in this battle*		509
The Wataree, S. C.	Aug. 15, 1780 (a surprise)	511
Fishing Creek, S. C.	**Aug. 18, 1780 (a surprise)**	512
Musgrove's Mills, S. C.	Aug. 18, 1780	518
Wahab's Plantation, S. C.	Sep. 20, 1780	518
Charlotte, N. C.	Sep. 26, 1780	519
Fish Dam Ford, S. C.	Nov. 9, 1780	521
Blackstock's Plantation, S. C.	Nov. 20, 1780 (a sharp action)	522
Charles City C. H., Va.	Jan. 8, 1781	540
McGowan's Ford, N. C.	Feb. 1, 1781	551
Allamance Creek	Feb. 25, 1781 (no quarter)	554
Wetzell's Mills, N. C.	Mar. 6, 1781 (a spirited action)	555
Petersburg, Va.	Apr. 25, 1781	589
Brandon, Va.	Apr. 25, 1781	589
Osborne, Va.	**Apr. 27, 1781**	590
Williamsburg, Va.	**June 16, 1781. (a sharp action)**	604
Quinby Bridge, S. C.	July 17, 1781	575
Monk's Corner, S. C.	July 17, 1781	575
Dorchester, S. C.	July 17, 1781	575
Gloucester, Va	October, 1781	636

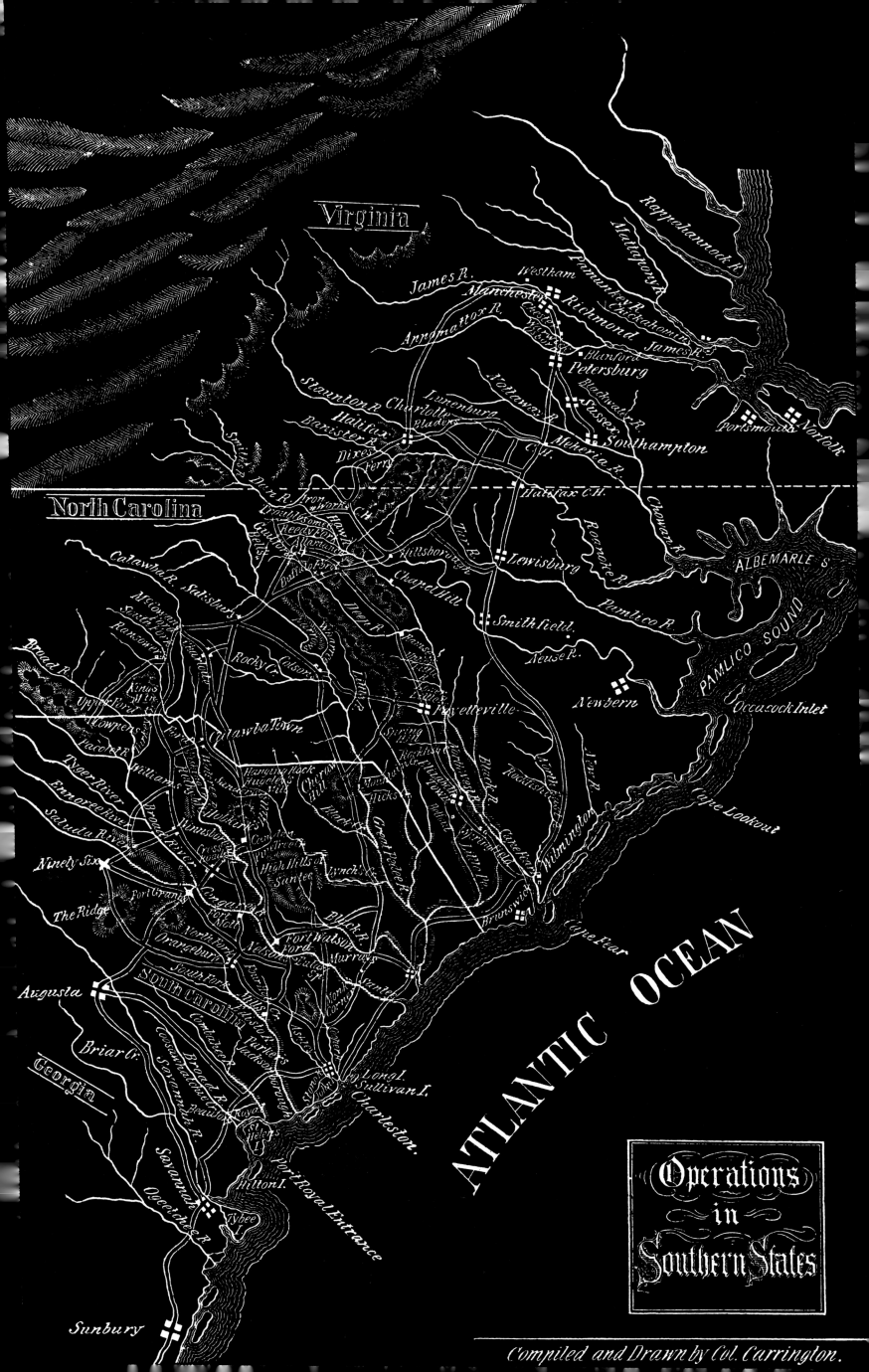

Operations in Southern States

Compiled and Drawn by Col. Carrington.

Battle of Guilford Court House

MARCH 15th, 1781

American Commanders
GREENE
Butler, Eaton, Ford, Col. Washington, Gunby, Kirkwood, Singleton, Williams, Huger, Stevens, Lee, Lynch, Hewes

Strength, 4,404   Casualties, 1,311

British Commanders
CORNWALLIS
Webster, O'Hara, Leslie, Norton, Tarleton McLeod, Howard

Strength, 1,800   Casualties, 554

MEM.—*The movements of the two armies had been such, that Greene selected Guilford Court House, for an issue with Cornwallis; and Cornwallis, as deliberately, resolved to attack the American army, whenever it offered battle.*

AMERICAN FORMATION.—The *first line*, 1,060 men (see map), was formed in the edge of woods, behind open ground, under cover of fences. From this point, the surface, quite thickly wooded, gradually ascended to the Court House, with hills on either side. Singleton placed his two guns on the road. Lynch's Rifles (200 men), Kirkwood's Delawares (80 men), and Washington's Dragoons, held the extreme *right*, to threaten the British *left*; while Lee's horse and the infantry of the Legion, with Campbell's Rifles, held the *left*, to threaten the British *right*.

The *second line*, 1,123 men (see map), was posted, 300 yards in the rear, with a few veterans, behind the line, to keep them up to duty.

The *third line*, 1,400 regulars, near the Court House, well posted, included Gunby's veteran regiment; but that of Ford, on the extreme left, was of new levies.

The map gives the divisions, by brigades.

BRITISH FORMATION.—*Right wing.* Bose (Hessian), and 71st regiment, with Leslie, commanding; 1st Guards (Norton) in reserve. *Left wing.* 23d and 33d regiments, under Webster; 2d Guards (General O'Hara) and Grenadiers in reserve. The Yagers and Light Infantry, to the left of the road, supported McLeod's guns. Tarleton's dragoons were in column, on the road, at the rear, to act as ordered.

Preliminary Skirmish.—Lee and Campbell were sent out by Greene, early in the morning, to feel the advancing enemy. In this skirmish, Captain Goodrick, of the British Guards, was killed, and nearly thirty of the Yagers and Dragoons were killed, or wounded. The Americans lost as many.

Development of the Battle

NOTE I.—As appears from the map, the American *first*, or advance line, over-lapped and attempted to flank the British line.

NOTE II.—Cornwallis urged the troops forward, in order to give full effect to their discipline; and rapidly combined the whole force in one line, which thereby equalled the American front. Lieut. O'Hara was killed at his guns, and the American wings delivered a hot fire; but the militia, in the *center*, gave way, in confusion, and Singleton took his guns to the rear, in their flight.

NOTE III.—The American *left* gains a wooded hill and holds the pursuing British *right* wing, to a separate, sharp engagement. The American right falls back in good order to the second line.

NOTE IV.—The *second* American line, resists bravely, but yields to pressure, and is put to flight, while Washington and Kirkwood, fall back in good order, to the reserves.

NOTE V.—At this stage of the action, the British assume, that success is no longer in doubt, and, that their entire progress, is to be unresisted. While the 71st regiment halts in the woods, to await a report from the rest of the right wing, which is engaged on the wooded hill, with Lee and Campbell, the 23d regiment halts, also. The extreme left wing was pushed directly for the American reserves, while the 2d Guards and Grenadiers, in like manner, moved impetuously to the front, without waiting for other support.

NOTE VI.—Gunby, and the left wing of Huger's brigade, meet the British left wing, with the bayonet, and drive them over a ravine to the west, where they remain, for a while, out of action.

NOTE VII.—The attack of the 2d Guards and Grenadiers was a surprise to Colonel Williams, of the American left wing, and both guns, which had been withdrawn to this point, were captured. Gunby, and, after his fall, Lt. Col. Howard, wheels the 1st Maryland, applies the bayonet, regains the guns, and repulses the attack. Washington's dragoons charge upon the disordered Guards. Stewart is killed, Gen. O'Hara is wounded, but rallies the Guards, and brings the 23d and 71st regiments into action. To cover their advance, the guns of McLeod are placed upon a knoll, near the wood, *which Singleton should have occupied in his retreat*, and Cornwallis pours fire into the American line, at risk to his own troops, which are not wholly disengaged from the American assault.

NOTE VIII.—When Gunby wheeled upon the Guards, the British left, under Webster, re-crossed the ravine and joined the main body.

NOTE IX.—Tarleton had dispersed Lee's horse, and with Bose's regiment and the 1st Guards, takes part in the action. The American left wing is overwhelmed, and Greene withdraws his army in good order, to Troublesome Creek, under cover of Colonel Green's regiment, which had remained nearly intact during the action. Cornwallis retired to Wilmington, N. C.

MEM.—*Tarleton says:* "*If the American artillery had pre-occupied the small hill by the roadside, the 23d and 71st could not have united with the Guards; and the result would have been fatal to the army of Cornwallis.*"

References:

CARRINGTON'S "BATTLES OF THE AMERICAN REVOLUTION," pp. 556-565.

School Histories:

Anderson, ¶ 107; p. 95.
Barnes, ¶ 2; p. 138.
Berard (Bush), ¶ 131; p. 174.
Goodrich, C. A.(Seaveys) ¶ 26; p. 142.
Goodrich, S. G., ¶ 8; p. 273.
Hassard, ¶ 14; p. 221.

Holmes, ¶ 8; p. 154-5.
Lossing, ¶ 6; p. 183-4.
Quackenbos, ¶ 390; p. 286-7.
Ridpath, ¶ 10; p. 223-4.
Sadlier (Excel.), ¶ 21; p. 205.
Stephens, A. H., ¶ 10; p. 225.

Swinton, ¶ 9; p. 158.
Scott, ¶ 7; p. 212.
Thalheimer (Eclectic), ¶ 291; p. 166.
Venable, ¶ 166; p. 127.

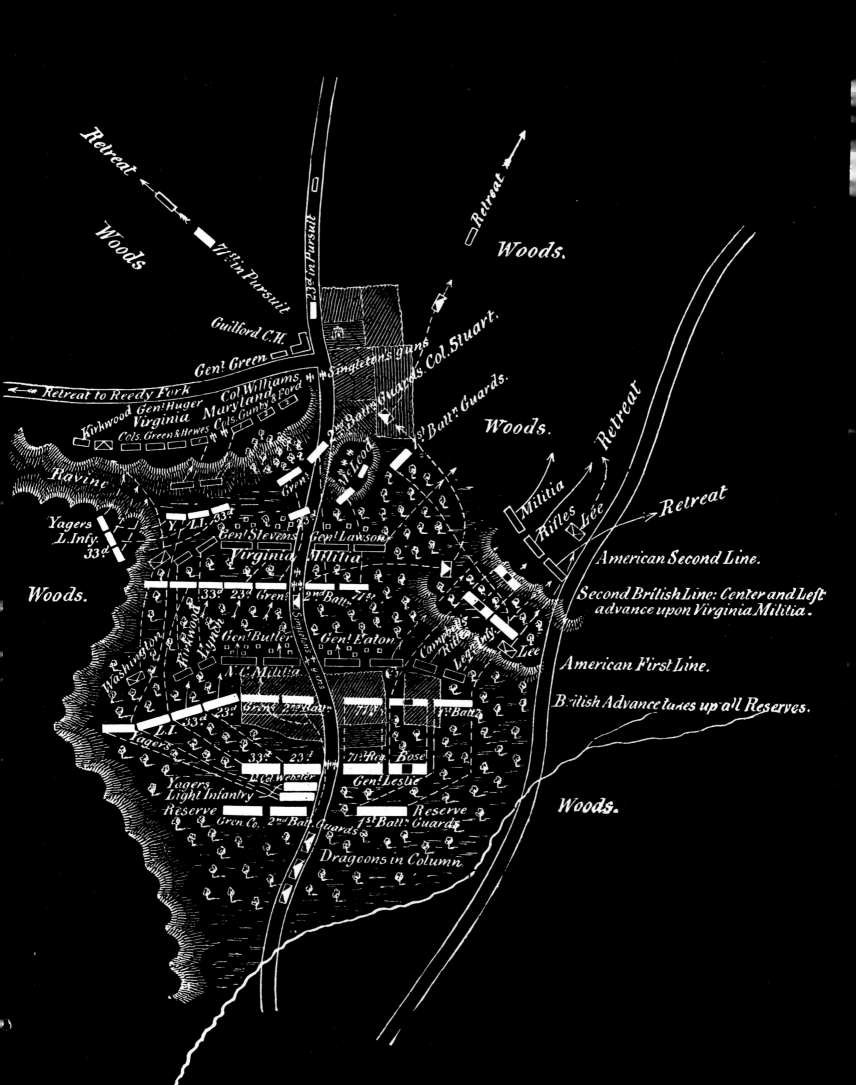

Battle of Guilford

	British
	Hessians.
	Dragoons.
	American.
	Horse.

Retreat

Woods

77th in Pursuit

23d in Pursuit

Woods.

Guilford C.H.

Gen! Green

Retreat to Reedy Fork

Kirkwood Gen! Huger   Col! Williams

Virginia   Maryland

Cols. Green & Hewes   Cols. Gumby & Ford

Singleton's guns

2nd Batt. Guards   Col. Stuart.

1st Batt. Guards.

Woods.

Retreat

Ravine

McLeod

Militia

Rifles   Lee

Retreat

Yagers
L. Infy.
33d

Y. L.I. 33d

Gen! Stevens   Gen! Lawson

Virginia   Militia

American Second Line.

Woods.

33d 23d Grens 2nd Batt. 77st.

Second British Line: Center and Left
advance upon Virginia Militia.

Washington

Kirkwood

Lynch

Gen! Butler   Gen! Eaton

N.C. Militia

Campbell's
Riflemen

Legn Infy

Lee

American First Line.

British Advance takes up all Reserves.

L.I. 33d 23d

Yagers

Grens 2nd Batt.   77th   1st Batt.

33d   23d

Br! Webster

71st Reg.   Bose

Gen! Leslie

Woods.

Yagers
Light Infantry
Reserve

Gren. Co. 2nd Batt. Guards   1st Batt. Guards

Reserve

Dragoons in Column.

Compiled and Drawn by Col. Carrington.

Battle of Hobkirk Hill

APRIL 25th, 1781

American Commanders
GREENE
Col. Washington, Williams, Campbell, Gunby, Ford, Hewes, Reade, Kirkwood, Benson, Morgan, Harrison, Beattie

Strength, 1,446   Casualties, 271

British Commanders
LORD FRANCIS RAWDON

Campbell   Robertson

Strength, 950   Casualties, 258

AMERICAN POSITION.—General Greene advanced to Log Town, within a short distance of Camden, April 19th, for the purpose of enticing Rawdon to an action ; but failing in this, and being too feeble to attack the post, he withdrew to Hobkirk Hill on the 24th. Upon a previous rumor, that Lieut.-Colonel Webster was on his way to reenforce Lord Rawdon, he had sent Colonel Carrington, with the artillery and baggage, back to Rugely's Mills. That officer had marched eight miles, when recalled, but did not regain camp until after 9 o'clock of the 25th. Greene had sent orders for Marion to join him ; but Rawdon, having learned from a deserter, of this order, and that the artillery had been sent to the rear, resolved to surprise the camp, without delay.

Hobkirk Hill is a narrow sand ridge, separating the head springs of small streams which flow to the Wateree and Pine Tree Creek. It was then thickly wooded, and abrupt, toward Camden. Woods also extended as far as Log Town, from which place, to Camden, the timber had been cleared, to prevent its use as cover for an approach to the post.

The American troops were at breakfast, when the alarm was given, of the approach of the British troops.

AMERICAN FORMATION.—The detachments of regular troops, then with Greene, had proved good soldiers, and he depended upon them fully. Huger took the right, with the regiments of Campbell and Hewes. The left wing, under Williams, consisted of the regiments of Gunby and Ford. The three guns, on their arrival, were masked in the centre, with orders for the supporting regiments to open their ranks after one discharge, then charge bayonet, and reserve their own fire until the ranks of the enemy were broken. The North Carolina militia, 250 men, under Colonel Reade, formed the reserve. In the belief that the assault would be made directly in front, orders were also given for the wings to wheel toward the advancing column, and thus concentrate a destructive cross-fire. Colonel Washington was to move toward Log Town at a gallop, and take Rawdon's forces in the rear. A small picket was also advanced a mile beyond the foot of the hill, under Kirkwood, Benson and Morgan.

BRITISH MOVEMENTS.—Rawdon placed the post in charge of convalescents, and so closely followed the line of swamp, to the eastward, in his march, that he gained the woods, unperceived by the Americans, until he met their pickets. A lively skirmish, first warned Greene of the movement, and led to the formation adopted. This route of march, however, carried the British troops to the left of the American lines, where the approach was easier, and the position less defensible.

The British troops formed, with the Sixty-third Regiment, the New York Volunteers and the King's Americans, as a first line, supported by the volunteers of Ireland and Captain Robertson's regiment, with the South Carolina regiment and fifty dragoons, as a reserve.

Lord Rawdon increased his front by the supports and reserves, as he advanced, to prevent the threatened movement upon his flank, and the action became general. The British line, thus hastily formed, as it advanced, began to give way under the pressure of the Americans, who began to descend the hill, as had been directed, in the plan of the battle.

Lieut.-Colonel Ford fell, severely wounded, and his men halted. Captain Beattie, on the right of Gunby's regiment, was mortally wounded. As the British pressed into the gap, Colonel Gunby made the grave mistake, of retiring the other companies, to reform the regiment. This gave the impression of retreat, and the Second Maryland Regiment fell back. Both rallied ; but it was too late. The British troops gained the summit, silenced the guns, and the retreat became general.

Meanwhile Colonel Washington had made his detour, taken paroles from wounded officers in the woods, gained some prisoners, and returned, to find the battle at an end.

The Americans saved their guns, which the British overlooked in their brief pursuit. Lord Rawdon states, that "the enemy's cavalry being superior to the British, their dragoons could not risk much," "and he would not suffer the infantry to break their order, for any benefit, that might be expected from a pursuit of the fugitives."

General Greene retired to Rugely's Mills,   Lord Rawdon fell back to Camden.

References:

CARRINGTON'S "BATTLES OF THE AMERICAN REVOLUTION," pp. 566–576.

School Histories:

Anderson, ¶ 108 ; p. 96.
Barnes, ¶ — ; p. —.
Berard (Bush), ¶ 132; p. 174-5.
Goodrich, C. A. (Seaveys), ¶ 27, p. 143.
Goodrich, S. G., ¶ 5; p. 273.
Hassard, ¶ 17 ; p. 222.

Holmes, ¶ 9 ; p. 155.
Lossing, ¶ 7 ; p. 184.
Quackenbos, ¶ 395 ; p. 289.
Ridpath, ¶ 11 ; p. 224.
Sadlier (Excel), ¶ — ; p. —.
Stephens, A. H. ¶ 11 ; p. 225-6.

Swinton, ¶ 10 ; p. 158.
Scott, ¶ 7 ; p. 212.
Thalheimer (Eclectic), ¶ — ; p. —.
Venable, ¶ 166 ; p. 127.

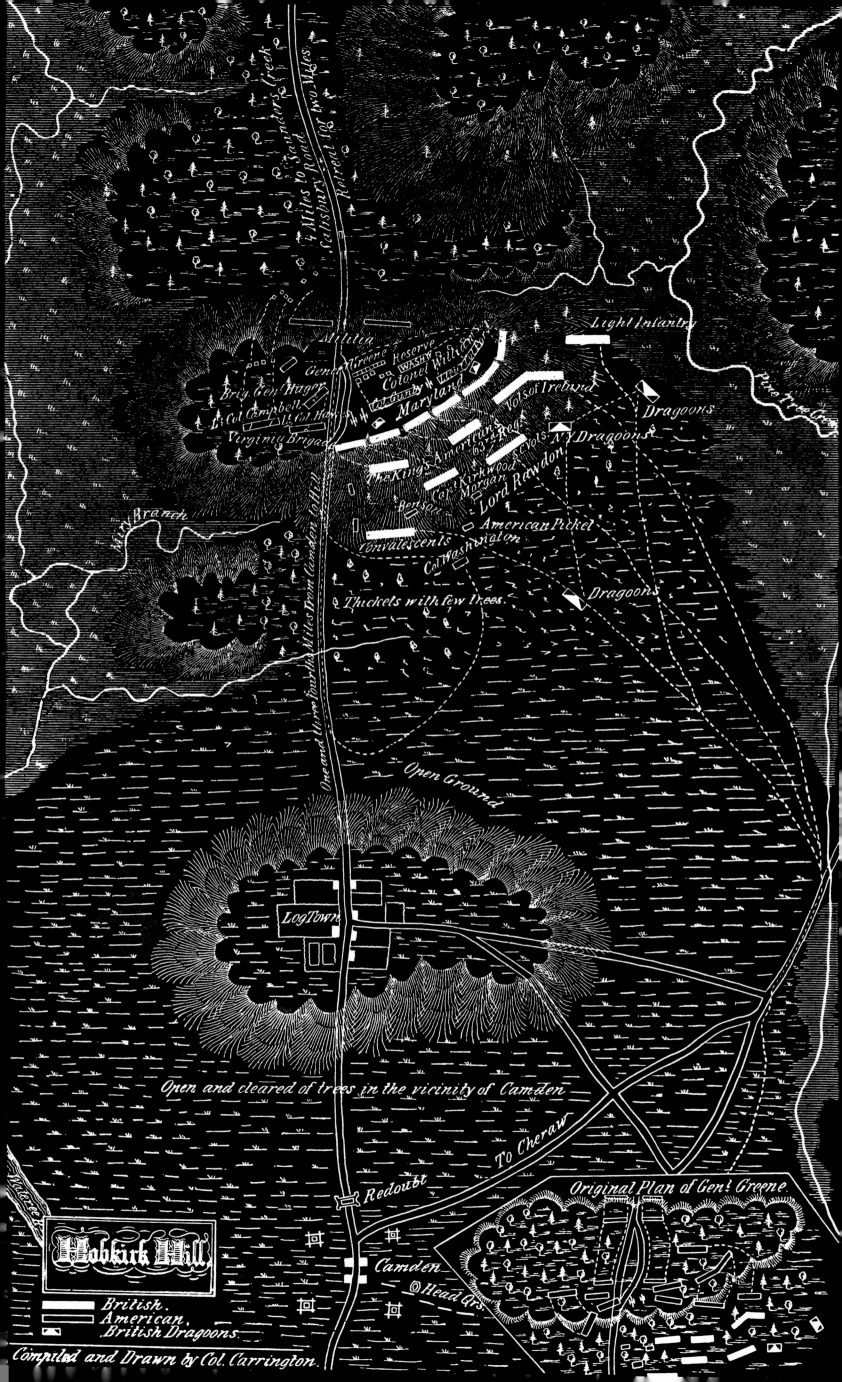

Militia

Gen. Greene Reserve
Brig. Gen. Huger Colonel Williams
Lt. Col. Campbell WASH
Lt. Col. Hawes company & maintain
Virginia Brigade Maryland

Light Infantry

Dragoons

The Kings Americans Vols of Ireland
63d Reg
Capt. Kirkwood S.C. vols N.Y. Dragoons
Morgan Lord Rawdon
Benson
American Picket
Convalescents
Col. Washington
Dragoons

Thickets with few trees

Open Ground

LogTown

Open and cleared of trees in the vicinity of Camden

To Cheraw

Redoubt

Original Plan of Genl. Greene.

Light Infantry

Hobkirk Hill.

—— British.
☐ American.
▽ British Dragoons.

Camden

Head Qrs.

Compiled and Drawn by Col. Carrington.

4 Miles to Saunders Creek

Salisbury Road Retreat for two Miles

One and three fourth Miles from Camden to Hill

Mary Branch

Pine Tree Creek

⇢ Battle of Eutaw Springs ⇠

SEPTEMBER 8th, 1781

American Commanders	British Commanders
GREENE	**STUART**
Sumner, Lee, Col. Washington, Henderson Marion, Kirkwood, Hampton, Ash, Campbell, Armstrong, Pickens, Blount Sweet, Williams, Malmady, Brown	Coffin. Majoribanks, Cruger, Sheridan
Strength, 2,400 Casualties, 408	Strength, 2,000 Casualties, 693

AMERICAN SITUATION.—General Greene rested his army at the High Hills of the Santee (see map. p. 72-3), was joined by General Sumner, with 700 Continental troops from North Carolina, and on Sept. 7th, encamped at Burdell's Plantation, on the Santee River, seven miles from Eutaw Springs. At 4 o'clock, A. M., September 8th, Greene marched to attack the British force at Eutaw Springs.

AMERICAN FORMATION.—"Front line, of four small battalions of militia, two of North, and two of South Carolina." Marion commanded the *right* wing, Pickens, the *left* wing, Colonel Malmady, the centre, with North Carolina militia, and two 3-pounders under Lieutenant Gaines. The *second* line consisted of three small brigades of Continental troops, of North Carolina, Virginia, and Maryland respectively, commanded by General Sumner, Colonel Campbell, and Colonel Williams. Captain Brown served two 6-pounders, on the road. Kirkwood's Delaware troops formed the reserve. Lieut.-Colonel Lee covered the right flank with his Legion horse, and Colonel Henderson, with the State troops, covered the left.

BRITISH SITUATION.— Stuart succeeded Rawdon in command at the South, with Head-quarters at Orangeburg, but fell back 40 miles, to Eutaw Springs, upon information that Lee, Marion, and Pickens, were concentrating their forces, under Greene. At 6 o'clock, A. M., September 8th, two deserters reported the situation of the American camp. The report was not credited. Major Coffin had been previously sent forward, with 150 men, to reconnoitre. A detachment from the British "Buffs," and their flanking battalions, had been sent out very early, as usual, to dig sweet potatoes, as they were plentiful, and bread was scarce, and no mills were near for grinding corn.

BRITISH FORMATION.— Stuart formed his line in advance of his tents, and with the purpose to offset, by position, the American superiority in mounted men. The *right* was toward Eutaw Creek, with Major Majoribanks, in a close thicket, nearly covered from sight. The 3d regiment "Irish Buffs," which only landed June 3d, constituted the right wing proper, with the American Royalists, under Lieut.-Colonel Cruger at the centre, and the 63d and 64th regiments on the *left*.

A small infantry detachment, with that of Captain Coffin, constituted a small reserve, covering the left flank of the camp, and the Charleston road ; while Major Sheridan, with some New York Volunteers, occupied a brick house, within a palisaded garden, which ultimately proved nearly as serviceable as did the Chew House at the battle of Germantown. Three guns "were distributed through the line." The field, occupied by both armies, was well wooded.

NOTES.

NOTE I.—Coffin met the American advance guard, nearly four miles from camp, and was driven in with a loss of 40 men. The "rooting parties," unarmed as they were, came in, much demoralized, leaving many prisoners in the hands of the Americans.

NOTE II.—Artillery firing began at 9 o'clock, with vigor, until one British piece and two American pieces were dismounted.

NOTE III.—"The British left wing," says Stuart, "by some unknown mistake, *advanced*, and drove the North Carolina militia before them, but unexpectedly finding the Virginia and Maryland line ready formed, and at the same time receiving a heavy fire, occasioned some confusion."

NOTE IV.—The North Carolina militia had fired seventeen rounds before retiring ; and Sumner sent his brigade so promptly to their support, that the British yielded. They renewed the attack, when supported by the reserve ; but the American reserve was pushed forward by Greene, and a bayonet charge, by Williams, broke the line.

NOTE V.—A sharp skirmish occurred at the right, where Majoribanks was posted. Colonel Henderson was wounded, and Lieut.-Colonel Wade Hampton succeeded to command of the cavalry on the American left. Washington and Kirkwood united in the attack. The thicket was so dense that Washington and 40 men were taken prisoners, and Majoribanks retired to the palisades of the garden.

NOTE VI.—Lee entered the British camp from its left, and   British fell back, to reform, obliquely, before the house.

NOTE VII.—Many American troops began to plunder the tents.

NOTE VIII.—Greene brought up his artillery, and attempted to restore order, and break the palisade defences ; but his gunners were shot down by fire from the windows (a house of three stories, as Greene reports), and leaving his guns, rather that sacrifice the men, he retired to Burdell's Plantation.

NOTE IX.—The 63d and 64th British, had served during the war, from the landing on Staten Island, in 1779.

NOTE X.—On the night of the 9th, Stuart retired to Monk's Corner, broke up, and threw in the river, 1,000 stand of arms, and left 70 wounded men to the care of the Americans.

MEM.—*This was the last formal engagement at the South.*

References :

CARRINGTON'S "BATTLES OF THE AMERICAN REVOLUTION," pp. 577-584.

School Histories:

Anderson, ¶ 109 ; p. 96.
Barnes, ¶ 2 ; p. 138.
Berard (Bush), ¶ — ; p. —.
Goodrich, C. A. (Seaveys), ¶ 28; p. 143.
Goodrich, S. G., ¶ 11 ; p. 274.
Hassard, ¶ 18 ; p. 222.

Holmes, ¶ 11 ; p. 156.
Lossing, ¶ 11 : p. 185-6.
Quackenbos, ¶ 399; p. 292-3.
Ridpath, ¶ 14 ; p. 224.
Sadlier, (Excel), ¶ 22 · p. 205.
Stephens, A. H. ¶ 14; p. 226-7.

Swinton, ¶ 12 ; p. 158.
Scott, ¶ 11 ; p. 214.
Thalheimer (Eclectic), ¶ 291 ; p. 166 ;
Venable, ¶ 166 ; p. 127.

Operations in Chesapeake Bay

THEIR SIGNIFICANCE

The effort to isolate the South, from the central colonies, came to an end with the surrender of Cornwallis in 1781.

From 1776, Virginia had been the scene of almost constant invasion and depredation.

As early as March 29th, 1777, General **Charles Lee**, then prisoner of war, in New York, thus addressed Admiral Howe and his brother, General Howe. " If the Province of Maryland, or the greater part of it, is reduced, or submits, and the people of Virginia are prevented or intimidated, from marching aid to the Pennsylvania army, the whole machine is divided, and a period put to the war; and if it (this plan,) is adopted in full, I am so confident of success that I would stake my life on the issue. Apprehensions from General Carleton's army will, I am confident, keep the New Englanders at home, or at least confine 'em to the east side of the river. I would advise that four thousand men be immediately embarked in transports, one-half of which should proceed up the Potomac, and take post at Alexandria; the other half up Chesaapeake Bay, and possess themselves of Annapolis."

Earl Cornwallis, when urging the transfer of his own operations from the Southern colonies, explicitly recognized the military importance of Chesapeake Bay, and that Virginia was the only base, subordinate to New York, from which to subjugate the South. He thus wrote to General Clinton, April 10th, 1781.

" I cannot help expressing my wishes that the Chesapeake may become the seat of war, even (if necessary) at the expense of abandoning New York. Until Virginia is, in a measure, subdued, our hold of the Carolinas must be difficult, if not precarious. The rivers of Virginia are advantageous to an invading army; but North Carolina is, of all the provinces in North America, the most difficult to attack (unless material assistance could be got from the inhabitants of the country, the contrary of which I have sufficiently experienced)—on account of its great extent, of its numberless rivers and creeks, and the total want of interior navigation."

On the 13th of April, he wrote to Lord Germaine : " The great reenforcements sent by Virginia to General Greene, whilst General Arnold was in the Chesapeake, are convincing proofs that small expeditions do not frighten that powerful province."

On the 21st of August, 1781, Washington, writing from Head Quarters, Kings Ferry, to Governor Livingston, thus confidentially disclosed his plans. (See Mag. Am. Hist., Feb. 1881, vol. IV, p. 141, and " Carrington's Battles," 4th Edition, p. 616, note).

Washington states therein, that " He intended to march in person, with the whole of the French army, and a detachment from the American army, with as much despatch as circumstances would admit, into Virginia, believing, that with the arrival of the Count De Grasse and his fleet, with a body of French troops on board, this would be the fairest opportunity to reduce the whole British force in the South, and ruin their boasted expectations in that quarter."

It was in the maturing events of 1781, that Washington disclosed the value of his early conception of the war, and its demands, and vindicated the wisdom of that strategy which he had so fully appreciated and enforced.

NOTE.—When the manœuvers of the French fleet led the British squadron into the offing, there to give battle, but thereby allowed the French fleet to enter from Rhode Island with siege guns for the land batteries, and then join De Grasse, and obtain absolute supremacy, it was plain that no adequate aid could come to Cornwallis, by sea; and the allied operations about New York, had assured Sir Henry Clinton that he could never again successfully invade New Jersey. The crowning military fact which attaches to the siege of Yorktown itself, is to be derived from the knowledge, that it was the culmination of that strategical conduct, by which Washington attested his character as a soldier throughout the war.

Mem.—Among the interesting facts to be associated with Chesapeake Bay, is this, that before Admiral Graves sailed for New York in 1781, the heaviest naval armament known to maritime warfare, viz: seventy-two hostile line-of-battle ships and heavy frigates, was floating on its surface.

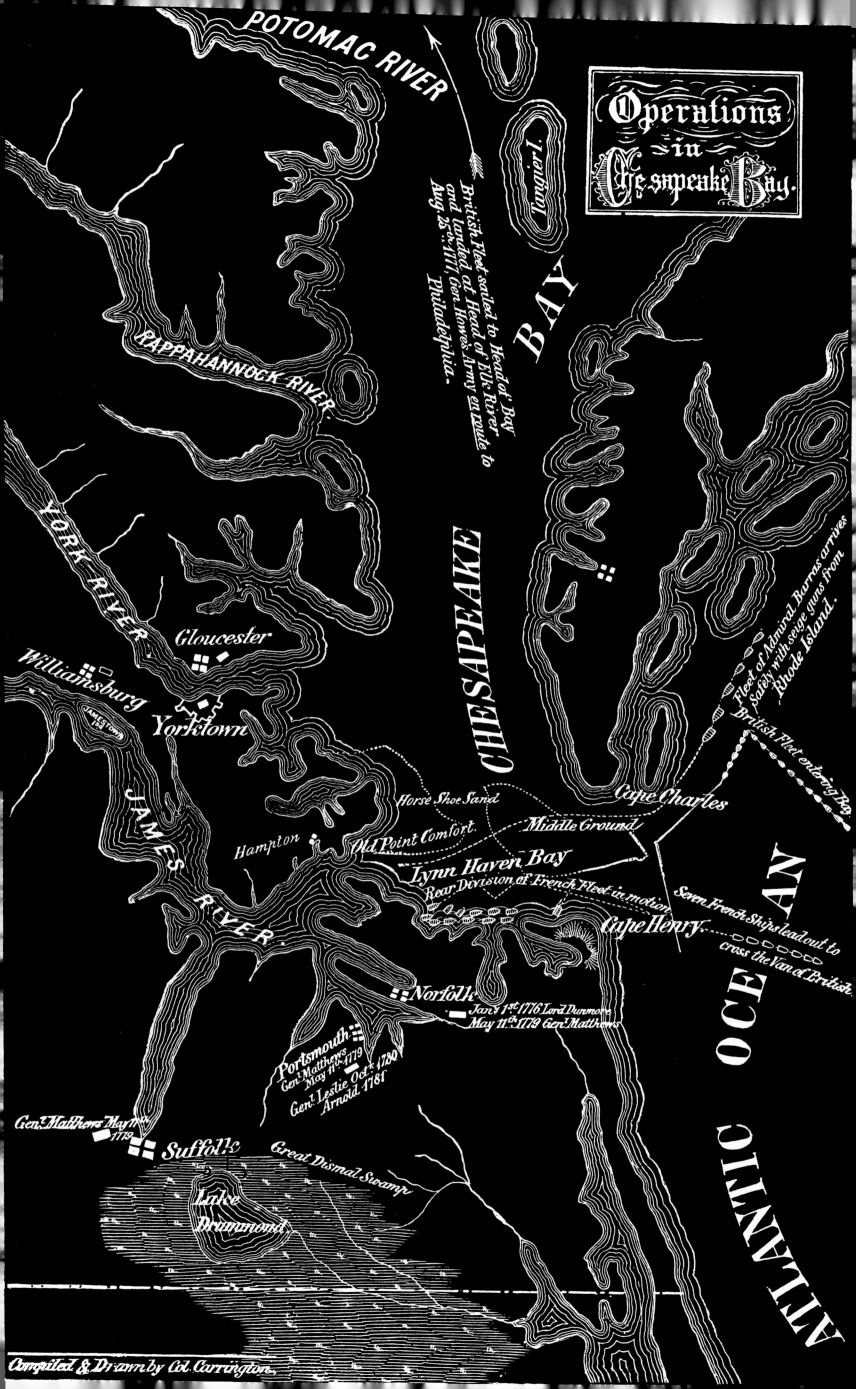

POTOMAC RIVER

Tangier I.

RAPPAHANNOCK RIVER

BAY

British Fleet sailed to Head of Bay
and landed at Head of Elk River,
Aug. 25th 1777, Gen. Howe's Army en route to
Philadelphia.

Operations
in
Chesapeake Bay.

YORK RIVER

Gloucester

Williamsburg

JAMESTOWN 1607

Yorktown

JAMES RIVER

CHESAPEAKE

Fleet of Admiral Barras arrives
safely with seige guns from
Rhode Island.

British Fleet entering Bay

Cape Charles

Horse Shoe Sand

Middle Ground

Hampton

Old Point Comfort.

Lynn Haven Bay
Rear Division of French Fleet in motion

OCEAN

Cape Henry.

Seven French Ships lead out to
cross the Van of British.

Norfolk

Jan.y 1st 1776 Lord Dunmore
May 11th 1779 Gen. Matthews

Portsmouth
Gen. Matthews
May 11th 1779
Gen. Leslie Oct. 1780
Arnold 1781

Gen. Matthews May 11th
1779

Suffolk

Great Dismal Swamp

Lake
Drummond

ATLANTIC

Lafayette in Virginia

American Commanders
LAFAYETTE
WAYNE   MUHLENBERG   STEUBEN

On the 18th of March, 1781, General Greene wrote thus, to Washington: "Could the Marquis (Lafayette) join us at this moment, we should have a glorious campaign. It would put Lord Cornwallis and his whole army into our hands."

On the 25th of April, Cornwallis left Wilmington, for Virginia, and Lafayette, who had reached Richmond, on the 29th, by a forced march from Baltimore, made plans, if reenforced in time, to anticipate the march of Cornwallis, and cut him off from union with Phillips. The reenforcements, seven hundred veterans, under Wayne, had been started southward by Washington, but were delayed in their march. On the 18th of May, Greene assigned Lafayette to the command in Virginia, but to "send all reports to the commander-in-chief" On the 25th of May, **Cornwallis was joined by General Leslie, with 2,278 fresh troops, which increased his force to 7,000 men, and he wrote to General Clinton, that " he should proceed to dislodge Lafayette from Richmond."**

British Commanders
CORNWALLIS
O'HARA   SIMCOE   TARLETON

PARALLEL NOTES

Note I.—The General Assembly adjourned to Charlottesville May 24th, and **Cornwallis crossed James River at Westover, on the 25th, encamping his whole army at White Oak Swamp on the 27th, in order to take Richmond in rear.** Lafayette, with a force less than one-third that of his adversary left the city northward, leading the British more than twenty miles.

Note II.—Cornwallis crossed the Chickahominy (see map), passed Hanover C. H., crossed the Pamunkey, then the North Anna, above New Found Creek, to head off the American column; but on the 29th, Lafayette still held the lead, crossed the North Anna, and was on his march to Spottsylvania Court House, in the supposed direction of Wayne's approach.

Note III.—**Cornwallis dropped the pursuit, sent Tarleton to Charlottesville, to attempt a capture of the General Assembly, and marched to Byrd Creek, where he joined Simcoe, and also Tarleton, upon return of the latter from Charlottesville.** The army, reunited, after forcing Steuben from his supply camp, at Elk Island, marched eastward, toward Richmond. Lafayette had been joined by Wayne, turned southward along Southwest Mountains, and by the 19th of June, when Steuben joined him, was marching parallel with the British army, the *pursued* having become the *pursuers.*

Note IV.—On the 23d of June, the American army had increased, by militia additions, to nearly 6,000 men, including 1,500 regulars. **The British had abandoned Richmond on the 20th, and on the 25th, Lafayette so hotly pressed their columns at Williamsburg, that the entire British army moved out to protect its rear.** Each army lost 30 men in the engagement.

On the 4th of July, the "Battle of Jamestown" was fought, the British losing 75, and the Americans 118; but Cornwallis crossed the James River, and Lafayette marched to Williamsburg and shut up the peninsula.

Note V.—**On the 9th of July, Tarleton made a fruitless raid (see map) to New London, Bedford County, and then joined Cornwallis, who took post at Yorktown, August 4th. By the 22d, the entire British army had concentrated at Yorktown and Gloucester.** Lafayette sent Wayne to cut off retreat, southward, and in urging Washington to come in person, and take command, concludes: "the British army must be forced to surrender. I heartily thank you for having ordered me to remain in Virginia. It is to your goodness that I am indebted for the most beautiful prospect I may ever behold."

Mem.—*The forced march to Richmond, skirmish at Williamsburg, the Battle of Jamestown and the weeks of rapid manœuvre, which wore out and shut up the army of Cornwallis, vindicate the confidence which Washington and Greene reposed in Lafayette; and the campaign, which Tarleton complimented in high terms, will stand, in history, as one of the most brilliant of the war.*

References:

CARRINGTON'S "BATTLES OF THE AMERICAN REVOLUTION," pp. 584–598.

School Histories:

Anderson, ¶ 110 ; p. 96.
Barnes, ¶ 2 ; p. 139.
Berard (Bush), ¶ — ; p. —.
Goodrich, C. A. (Seaveys), ¶ 30, p. 141.
Goodrich, S. G., ¶ 1-2; p. 276.
Hassard, ¶ 9 ; p. 226.

Holmes, ¶ 12 ; p. 157.
Lossing, ¶ 13 ; p. 186.
Quackenbos, ¶ 400 ; p. 294.
Ridpath, ¶ 17 ; p. 226.
Sadlier (Excel), ¶ 23 ; p. 206.
Stephens, A. H. ¶ 15; p. 227-8.

Swinton, ¶ — ; p. —.
Scott, ¶ — ; p. —.
Thalheimer (Eclectic), ¶ —; p. —.
Venable, ¶ 167 ; p. 128.

Lafayette
in
Virginia

Compiled and Drawn by Col. Carrington.

Benedict Arnold at New London

SEPTEMBER 6th, 1781

On the 6th day of September, 1781, the twenty-fourth birthday of Lafayette, and while Washington and Rochambeau were hastening to join the Army of Virginia, and consummate plans for the rescue of that Colony and the capture of Cornwallis, it was left to General Clinton to express his chagrin at thorough out-generalship, by a raid into Connecticut, under the traitor Arnold.

The expedition left New York, September 4th, and entered the harbor of New London, at half-past six in the morning, two days later. According to Arnold's Official Report, the landing was effected on both sides of the harbor, about nine o'clock, September 6th.

As a diversion, to annoy Washington, it was trifling; if so intended. He never swerved from general plans, for small local issues. As a military movement, it contemplated no battle, no substantial resistance ; and, while it might plunder and destroy, it could only intensify opposition to Great Britain. As a matter of military policy, it was wretched, since Arnold, the traitor, was sent to lay waste his own birthplace.

New London Defences

FORT TRUMBULL, on the New London bank of the Thames River, was a mere breastwork, or water battery, almost open, landward. Just west of this, on high ground, a small redoubt had been established, but it bore the name, " Fort Folly," or " Fort Nonsense, and had no defenders, Fort Trumbull, itself, was occupied by not more than thirty men, State troops, under Captain Adam Shapley.

FORT GRISWOLD, which crowned the height on the east shore, was a well conceived redoubt, with parapet, bastions, a covered entrance, a well of water, and was supplemented by a small advanced redoubt, slightly down the hill, and this connected by a close passage with the main work. The garrison was less than 160 men, under Lieut. Colonel Ledyard. A small knoll, or ledge, called Avery's Hill, was to the northeast, but while not commanding the works, was a place for the lodgment of assailants. and was finally occupied by the invaders.

British Movements

ARNOLD conducted the left wing, or column, which burned the town. It consisted of 4 companies of the 38th regiment, under Captain Millett ; a detachment of Yagers, with two 6-pounder guns, a portion of the Legion of Loyal Americans. and 120 "American Refugees," under Captain Frink, from Long Island.

NOTE I.—Millett advanced upon Fort Trumbull, and received a volley which disabled several men; but the small command of Shapley, took boats for Fort Griswold, losing several men, in one boat, which was shattered by a ball, but joining its garrison.

NOTE II.—When Arnold reached New London, and saw the escape of Shapley, and the defensive condition of Fort Griswold, he sent orders to Lieut. Colonel Eyre, countermanding the movement on the east side; but too late, as the advance had been made. His own movements were confined to the unresisted destruction of property. He burned ten or twelve ships, with their stores, one of which, the Hannah, from London, recently captured as a prize by the Americans, contained powder. Arnold claimed that the fire which burned 65 dwellings, 35 stores and warehouses. 80 ships, 20 barns, a meeting-house, court-house, jail, market-house, and custom-house, was the result of the explosion of powder, and a change of wind, which " unfortunately destroyed, notwithstanding efforts to prevent it."

The Right Wing or Column

LIEUT. COL. EYRE landed, back of Pine Island, and advanced in two divisions, the 54th and 40th regiments, respectively, leading each. One gun and one howitzer accompanied the command. The right division was supported by a detachment of Yagers, and the left division, by New Jersey Volunteers ; but the last named fell behind, while making the circuit of swampy ground. and did not rejoin, until the storming party mounted the rampart.

CAPT. BECKWITH, who bore from Eyre to Ledyard, a demand for surrender of the fort, received, through Captain Shapley, the prompt rejection of terms. The prompt reenforcement of the fort by militia, who were available, and partially depended upon, in the debate as to the demand for surrender, might have assured a final repulse. Better defences than at Breed's Hill, in 1775, covered the defenders; but although Colonel Nathan Gallup, of the Groton militia, had faith in his ability to fill the fort with men, they would not consent to be enclosed by works, with no avenue for escape. The real battle was quickly fought. The storming parties on the south and southeast, were compelled to pass a deep ditch, and climb an embankment of twelve feet. Those from the east, entered through three embrasures in the rampart. flanking the salient angle. The Yagers passed around. nearly to the gate. The first repulse inflicted a slaughter of the assailants, greater than the number of the garrison. The *second assault* crowned the parapet. Eyre and three other officers had been wounded, and Major Montgomery was killed by a spear, so that Major Broomfield, a New Jersey Loyalist, took command in the final charge with bayonets. Lieut. Colonel Buskirk, of the New Jersey Volunteers, came up tardily. but participated in the assault.

Lieut. Colonel Ledyard ordered the gate opened, and, fairly surrendered the fort ; but nothing would satisfy the tory allies of the British troops, but wholesale slaughter of the brave defenders. Eighty-five men were found dead, and sixty were dangerously wounded. The American loss, up to the moment of a fair surrender. had been trifling.

The British loss was severe, having been officially reported as " one Major," one Captain, one Lieutenant, two Ensigns, two Sergeants, and forty rank and file killed ; and one Lieut. Colonel, two Captains, one Lieutenant, one Ensign, eight Sergeants, two drummers, and one hundred and twenty-seven wounded ; making total casualties. one hundred and sixty-three.

References:

CARRINGTON'S " BATTLES OF THE AMERICAN REVOLUTION," pp. 625-630

School Histories :

Anderson, ¶ 113 ; p. 97.
Barnes, ¶ Note ; p. 140.
Berard (Bush), ¶ 137 ; p. 176.
Goodrich, C.A.(Seaveys),¶ —; p. —.
Goodrich, S. G., ¶ 6 ; p. 271.
Hassard, ¶ 7 ; p. 225.

Holmes, ¶ 15 ; p. 158.
Lossing, ¶ 15 ; p. 187.
Quackenbos,¶ 400; p. 294.
Ridpath ¶ 5 ; p. 242.
Sadlier (Excel).¶ —; p. —.
Stephens, A. H.¶ —; p. —.

Swinton, ¶ —; p. —.
Scott, ¶ 15 ; p. 215.
Thalheimer (Eclectic), ¶ 295; p. 171-2.
Venable, ¶ —; p. —.

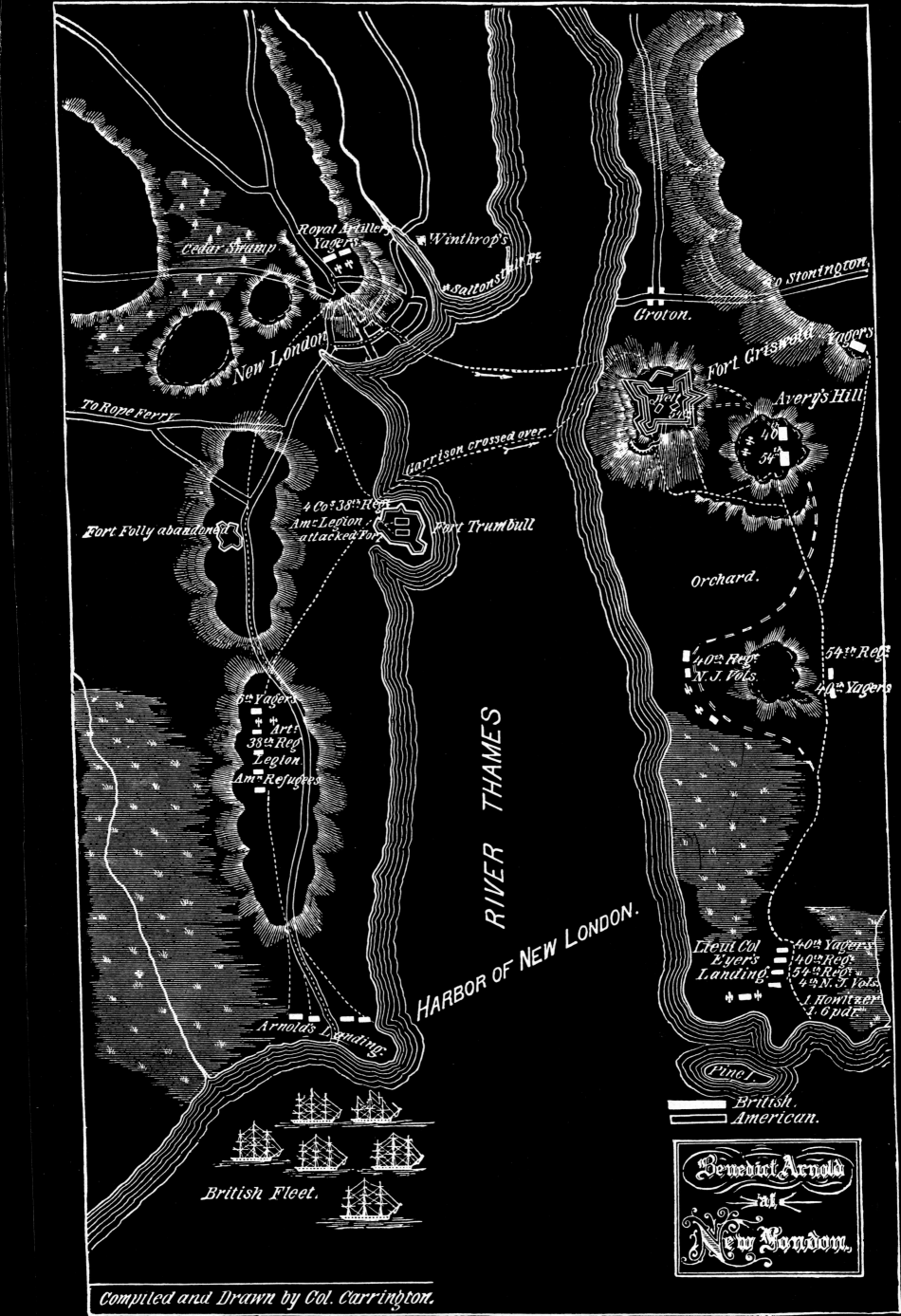

Royal Artillery
Yagers
Cedar Swamp
✠ Winthrop's
⊹ Saltonstall Pt.

New London

To Rope Ferry

To Stonington
Groton.

Fort Griswold Yagers
Avery's Hill

Garrison crossed over

Fort Folly abandoned

4 Co. 38th Reg.
Am. Legion
attacked Fort
Fort Trumbull

Orchard.

40th Regt.
N. J. Vols.
54th Reg.
40th Yagers

6th Yagers
✠ Art.
38th Reg.
Legion.
Am. Refugees

RIVER THAMES

HARBOR OF NEW LONDON.

Lieut Col
Eyer's
Landing.
40th Yagers
40th Reg.
54th Reg.
4th N. J. Vols.
✠ 1 Howitzer
1. 6 pdr.

Arnold's Landing.

Pine I.

British.
American.

British Fleet.

*Benedict Arnold
at
New London.*

Compiled and Drawn by Col. Carrington.

❧ Siege of Yorktown, 1781 ❧

Strength of Allied Forces, 16,400
GEORGE WASHINGTON
Commander-in-Chief

American Forces	French Forces
MARQUIS DE LAFAYETTE	Lieut.-Gen. COUNT DE ROCHAMBEAU
General LINCOLN	" and Admiral COUNT DE GRASSE
" WAYNE	Admiral COUNT DE BARRAS
" KNOX	General DE BEVILLE
" DU PORTAIL	" BARON DE VIOMENIL
" BARON STEUBEN	" MARQUIS DE CHASTELLUX
" NELSON	" M. DE CHOISY
" WEEDON	Chevalier Colonel DE LAMETH
" CLINTON	Colonel COUNT DE DUMAS
" ST. CLAIR	" COUNT DE DEUX PONTS
" LAWSON	" GIMAT
" MUHLENBERG	General DUKE DE LAUZUN
Colonel HAMILTON	" DE ST. SIMON
" STEVENS LAMB	MARQUIS DE LA ROUERIE
" CARRINGTON	MARQUIS DE L. MONTMORENCI
" SCAMMEL	MARQUIS DE SAINT MAIME
" LAURENS	MARQUIS DE CUSTINE

INTRODUCTORY NOTE

Washington and Rochambeau pressed Lieut. General Clinton, British commander, at New York, so closely, that he believed that their *feints* were real movements. and called upon Cornwallis to send troops to *resist a threatened siege* of New York. August 25th. The allied armies were west of Hudson River, but *not* to attack Staten Island or New York. September 2d, the American army, and September 3d, the French army, swept swiftly through Philadelphia. On the 5th, while passing Chester, Washington learned from a courier, that Count de Grasse was off the coast.; and on the 14th, he was at Lafayette's headquarters, at Williamsburg, Va.

British Commanders
EARL CORNWALLIS, Lieut.-General

O'HARA   SIMCOE   TARLETON

Strength, 8,525

NOTE I.—Washington, asking on the 15th. for transportation for his troops, from head of Elk River, found, that Admiral de Barras had already sent ships for that purpose. On the 18th, with Rochambeau, Knox, and Du Portail, he visited De Grasse, upon his flagship, "La Ville de Paris."

NOTE II.—September 25th, the army (12,400 regulars, and 4,000 militia) concentrated, at Williamsburg; took position, within two miles of British advanced works, on the 28th and, after reconnoisance in force, on the 29th environed Yorktown. Colonel Scammel was mortally wounded; **British out-works were abandoned.** Lincoln occupied the banks of Wormley Creek, near the Moore House. (See map, for location of besieging forces).

NOTE III.—On the Gloucester side, Duke de Lauzun, with his cavalry; Weedon's Virginia militia, and 600 French marines, all under General de Choisy, held the Neck, cutting off retreat northward. **Tarleton's last exploit, was in a collision with Lauzun's dragoons, in which he was unhorsed.**

NOTE IV.—October 6th, heavy guns were brought up, and the first parallel was opened, 600 yards from the lines, under Lincoln. On the 7th and 8th, guns were mounted on the works, which the British had previously abandoned..

At 5 P. M., October 9th, the Americans, on the right, opened fire, with six 18 and 24-pounders, two mortars, two howitzers; and the French opened fire, on the left. with four 12-pounders, and six howitzers. On the 10th, two French. and two American batteries, opened fire from ten 18 and 24-pounders, and eight mortars, One hot shot burned the frigate Charon (44).

NOTE V.—October 11th, the second parallel was begun, within 300 yards. October 14th, it became necessary to silence two redoubts, next the river. A column, organized by Lafayette, with Hamilton as immediate commander, and one organized by Baron de Viomenil, with Count Deux Ponts, as immediate commander. stormed the redoubts, at one rocket signal, at night, with perfect success. Laurens supported Hamilton, and in the assault, Colonels Gimat, Barber, Count de Dumas, Chevalier de Lameth, and Count de Deux Ponts, were wounded. At left of parallel, marked F, a ravine answered for a covered approach. (It was also utilized by Colonel Poe, United States Engineer, in 1862.)

NOTE VI.—**On the 19th of October,** pursuant to articles, signed, on the 18th, by Cornwallis and Symonds, at Yorktown; and by Washington, Rochambeau, and De Barras (for himself and De Grasse), "in the trenches, before Yorktown, in Virginia." **the surrender of the British army and post was completed.**

NOTE VII.—*American* casualties, 33 killed, 65 wounded; *French*, 52 killed, 134 wounded. *British*, 156 killed, 326 wounded, and 70 missing. Force surrendered, Officers and men, 7,073, and of seamen and shipping, 900.

References:

CARRINGTON'S "BATTLES OF THE AMERICAN REVOLUTION," pp. 631–647.
School Histories:

Anderson, ¶ 114; p. 97.	Holmes, ¶ 13; p. 227.	Swinton, ¶ 4; p. 158.
Barnes, ¶ 3; p. 139-40.	Lossing, ¶ 16; p. 187-8.	Scott, ¶ 16-18; p. 216.
Berard (Bush), ¶ 140; p. 177.	Quackenbos, ¶ 400-2; p. 293-5.	Thalheimer (Eclectic), ¶ 303-6;
Goodrich,C.A.(Seaveys),¶ 33-4, p.145.	Ridpath, ¶ 18; p. 226.	p. 175-6.
Goodrich, S. G., ¶ 4-9; p. 277-8.	Sadlier (Excel), ¶ 16-18; p. 214.	Venable, ¶ 167; p. 128-9.
Hassard, ¶ 13; p. 227.	Stephens, A.H. ¶ 18; p. 229.	

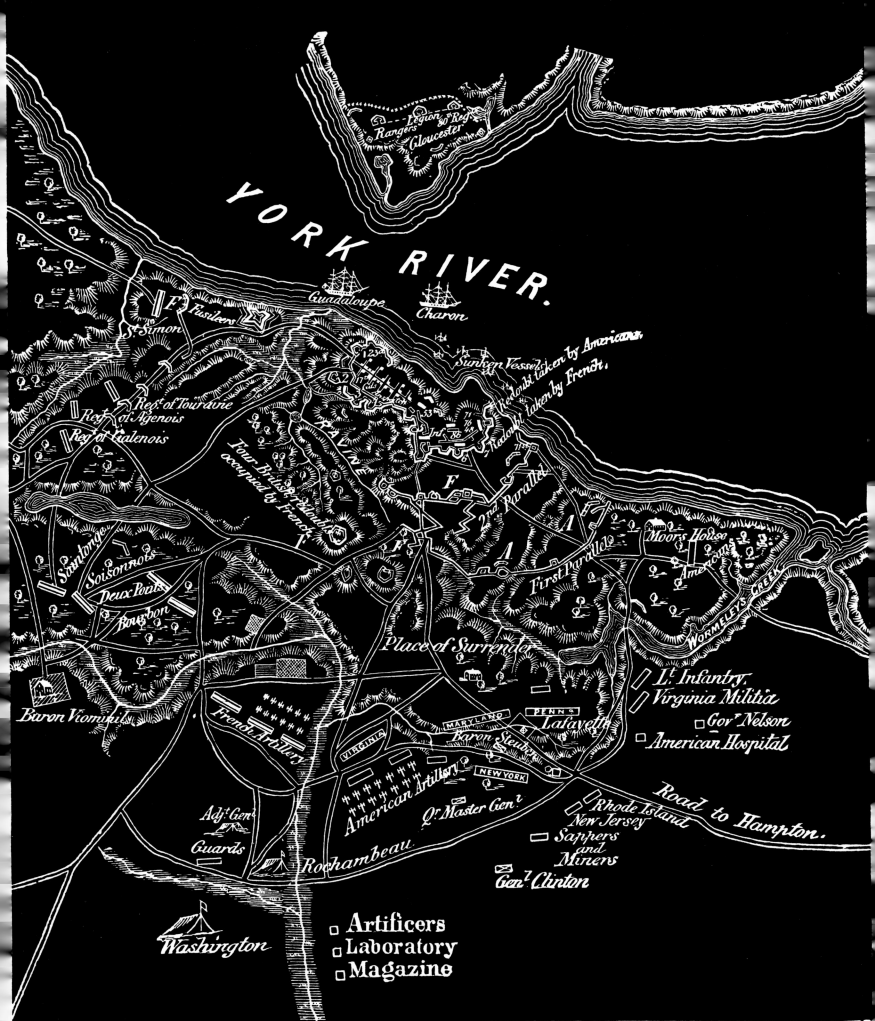

Siege of Yorktown.

American.
French.
British.

YORK RIVER.

Legion
Rangers
80ᵗʰ Regᵗ
Gloucester

Fˢ Fusilers
Guadaloupe
Charon
Sᵗ Simon

Regᵗ of Touraine
Regᵗ of Agenois
Regᵗ of Gatenois

Four British Redoubts occupied by French

Sunken Vessel taken by Americans
Redoubt taken by French
Redoubt taken by French

2ⁿᵈ Parallel

Saintonge
Soissonnois
Deux Ponts
Bourbon

Moors House
First Parallel
Americans
WORMELEYS CREEK

Place of Surrender

Baron Viomenil
French Artillery
MARYLAND
VIRGINIA
Baron Steuben
American Artillery
NEW YORK
Qʳ Master Genˡ
Lafayette
PENN
Lᵗ Infantry.
Virginia Militia
Govʳ Nelson
American Hospital

Rhode Island
New Jersey
Sappers and Miners
Genˡ Clinton
Road to Hampton.

Adjᵗ Genˡ
Guards
Rochambeau

Washington

☐ Artificers
☐ Laboratory
☐ Magazine

Compiled and Drawn by Col. Carrington

Summary of Events

The War for American Independence

Had its true policy declared by Gen. NATHANIEL GREENE, then in camp before Boston, during June, 1775. It was this, in brief :

(SEE CARRINGTON'S "BATTLES OF THE AMERICAN REVOLUTION," pp. 80-91.)

1. One General-in-Chief.
2. Enlistments, for the war.
3. Bounties, for families of soldiers in the field.
4. Service, to be general, regardless of place of enlistment.
5. Money loans to be effected, equal to the demands of the war.
6. A Declaration of Independence, with the pledge of all the resources, of each Colony, to its support.

Original Army Organization

GEORGE WASHINGTON
Commander-in-Chief

HORATIO GATES
Adjutant General

Major Generals
(RANKING AS NAMED)
ARTEMAS WARD   CHARLES LEE   PHILIP SCHUYLER
ISRAEL PUTNAM

Brigadier Generals
SETH POMEROY, RICHARD MONTGOMERY, DAVID WOOSTER
WILLIAM HEATH, JOSEPH SPENCER
JOHN THOMAS,   NATHANIEL GREENE.

Declaration of Independence
JULY 4th, 1776

Surrender of Cornwallis
OCTOBER 19th, 1781

Cessation of Hostilities
OFFICIALLY DECLARED, APRIL 18th, 1783